San Francisco
A CERTAIN STYLE

San Francisco
A CERTAIN STYLE

BY DIANE DORRANS SAEKS

PHOTOGRAPHY BY JOHN VAUGHAN

FOREWORD BY HERB CAEN

BOOK DESIGN BY LAURA LAMAR

CHRONICLE BOOKS

SAN FRANCISCO

Library of Congress Cataloging-in-Publication Data:
Saeks, Diane Dorrans.
*San Francisco : A Certain Style / Diane Dorrans Saeks ;
photography by John Vaughan.*
p. cm.
Includes index.
ISBN 0-8118-0199-3
*1. Interior decoration—California—San Francisco—
History—20th century. 2. Interior architecture—
California—San Francisco--History—20th century.
I. Vaughan, John, 1952-   . II. Title*

NK2004. S24 1989   89-17299
728' .09794'61—dc20   CIP

*The author and photographer gratefully acknowledge the
editors of* Architectural Digest, Metropolitan Home, Home,
House Beautiful, *and* Victoria *for use of photographs previously published in those magazines.*

*The photographer thanks Claire Marie for the flowers at the
Rosekrans residence. For years of processing his film, he also
thanks Faulkner Color Lab.*

*Book and cover design by Laura Lamar; calligraphic
letterforms by Max Seabaugh, MAX, San Francisco.
Produced on the Macintosh using Letraset's Ready,Set,Go!
and Adobe type families Palatino and Futura.
Type output at Digital Pre-Press International; special thanks
to Sanjay and Janet Sakhuja and Lauraine Woods.*

*Distributed in Canada by:
Raincoast Books
112 East Third Street
Vancouver, B.C.
V5T 1C8*

10 9 8 7 6 5 4 3

*Chronicle Books
275 Fifth Street
San Francisco, California
94103*

Printed in Hong Kong.

**Photograph on half-title
page:** Russell MacMasters's
elegant synthesis of East and
West, photographed in his
studio. The Japanese lantern is
a MacMasters design.

Previous page: Whitney
Warren's legendary house on
Telegraph Hill, empty
save for a taste of the dramatic
architectural details and
antiques that formerly graced
the rooms.
Architect: Gardner Dailey.

Table of Contents

Photographs on following pages:
Fogscape (page 6): Sutro Tower sails through incoming fog, viewed from architect Darwin McCredie's garden. His renovated attic apartment is visible within.
Cityscape (pages 10-11): The spires of the City from Potrero Hill. Controversial new structures have changed the skyline forever but handsome old downtown buildings of character and strength still stand as reminders of an elegant past.
Roofscape (pages 12-13): Cow Hollow and Pacific Heights from Charlotte Swig's sunny terrace.
Tablescape (pages 14-15): Arts patrons John and Dodie Rosekrans surround themselves with art, flowers, and objects to please the senses. Designer Michael Taylor's ploy: Fill their smoking room with large-scale sculpture, opulent chairs, curious minerals to make it appear dramatically larger.

Acknowledgements

John and I had the very best time choosing, photographing, and writing about the houses of San Francisco. We wish to acknowledge all of the San Francisco designers and architects whose ideas are lavished on the rooms in these pages. Our warmest thanks, too, to the owners of the houses—from Nob Hill to the Mission and over to Pacific Heights, from the Alexander Valley to Hillsborough. ¶ To Herb Caen, San Francisco chronicler, thanks for a picture-perfect foreword. ¶ To Dorothy Kalins, Carol Helms, Ben Lloyd, Steven Wagner, Barbara Graustark, Arlene Hirst, Newell Turner, and all our wonderful friends at *Metropolitan Home*—cheers and thanks for being the best. ¶ Heartfelt thanks to Paige Rense, Editor-in-Chief of *Architectural Digest,* for her many years of generosity and support. ¶ Andree Putman has encouraged us in this book from the very beginning. Our grateful thanks and respect. ¶ Warm thanks to Margaret Kennedy, Executive Editor of *House Beautiful.* ¶ Thanks to Russell McMasters and Robert Steffy for inspiration, generosity, and warm friendship. Maria Gresham and Perry Klehbahn have been the very finest assistants. ¶ To Nion McEvoy, David Barich, Jack Jensen, Annie Barrows, and the staff at Chronicle Books—our appreciation for enthusiasm and openness to our ideas. ¶ Fred Hill has been a wonderful agent. ¶ To our editor, Terry Ryan, thanks for the best encouragement and humor, and for the keen editing eye. ¶ To Ron Mann and Steven Mann, Geraldine Paton, and Gwyneth Dorrans for always being there. ¶ And an especially warm round of applause to our book designer, Laura Lamar. Her caffè lattes at the light box, Max, merry laughter, and the Mac made light work and marvelous layouts.

Diane Dorrans Saeks
John Vaughan

To my son, Justin, with love.

In fond memory of John Dickinson, friend and mentor.

D.D.S.

To Mom and Dad.

J.E.V.

Foreword

Junky houses at the end of junky alleys, secret gardens behind blank-faced mansions that turn a cold shoulder to the world, flower-like Southeast Asian children playing innocently in the Tenderloin, a cable car inching crookedly down Washington toward Powell, where the view opens suddenly to Bay-Bridge'd magnificence. ❡ It's a City, all right, a nervous place built on jitters and fidgets and filled-in land. It could go any minute, slipping and sliding into the enigmatic bay. A lot of it is gone already—the city of forgotten people who led fabulous lives in houses built for the ages disappeared long ago. Myths and legends have died, with nobody left to remember. Ghostly dance music in the marble halls of ancient hotels, Cape Jasmine gardenias turning brown, faded photos of people from another time, smiling around a supper club table, each with a cigarette in one hand, a glass of rotgut in the other. The dashing, debonair royalty of another San Francisco with their Stutz Bearcats and plus fours and white teeth in faces forever tanned. They had style and money to burn, and their snobby manners were impeccable, old boy. ❡ I wander around the city, rubbing shoulders with ghosts, trying to find the pieces. Up to Twin Peaks, where a giant statue of St. Francis by Beniamino Bufano was planned and forgotten; but once there was a giant Christmas tree every December. Past Red Rock in the Sunset, where the young Saroyan sat and looked out at the shining sea. Out to the Cliff House, a shadow of the magnificence that Mayor Adolph Sutro gazed down on from his garden-girt mansion on the bluffs. "In San Francisco," Saroyan once said in an excess of ebullience, "even the ugly is beautiful," and I know what he meant as I drive past the odd little houses on the silent streets of the outer avenues, a study in photo-realism, every block different but alike. Clement, Irving, Balboa, the heartland of the city, the stores and restaurants marching into infinity. ❡ If you can avert your eyes from certain difficult realities, the city is looking good, fat, prosperous, and preposterously glamorous. Van Ness aglow with operas and ballets and symphonies and parties. The days are short and the nights are long, always the perfect proportions for a city that has played hard from birth. The merry-go-round spins even faster, and "Laughin' Sal" cackles madly, the uninvited guest at the never-ending banquet of Baghdad-by-the-Bay.

. . . Herb Caen

When he's not at the "Loyal Royal" writing his popular six-days-a-week column for the *San Francisco Chronicle*, Herb Caen may be at home in his comfortable Nob Hill apartment, *above and opposite*. Interior design: Billy Gaylord with Andrew Lau.

Introduction

John Dickinson, who design professionals consider one of the most original and influential American designers, was my first inspiration for this book. ¶ In the late sixties, well before High Tech, Dickinson designed a steel-pipe four-poster bed for artist Ralph Du Casse, wrapped it with walls of charcoal-and-white herringbone tweed, and covered it luxuriously with pure camel-hair originally intended for menswear. ¶ In Dr. Leo Keoshian's Peninsula house, sumptuous but spare furniture of Dickinson's design was showcased in creamy white rooms. *Faux primitif* animal-footed tables and chairs, glossy white epoxyed tables, a grand stainless-steel bath standing alone in the center of an all-white bathroom are pure Dickinson. ¶ In 1980, I started work on a book about John's designs. I'd been writing about interior design and fashion since my first year at university, but this was to be my real education. At nine every Sunday morning, I'd arrive at John's Washington Street firehouse, with its brass name plates and white-canvas-duck-curtained portiere. Climbing the stairs worn to a beautiful patina by decades of firemen, I'd hear bouncy Cole Porter from John's Steinway. Throwing open the ten-foot-high white-lacquered doors at the top of the stairs, I would see John across the room playing the piano in his starched white Sulka pajamas. Sun streaming through brass-bound window shutters turned his white hair into a halo. He was always smiling. ¶ This sky-lit living room (shown on page 50) was so dramatic in size and in its particular pieces that a visit was never mundane. There was Dickinson's collection of African figures mounted in groups on white plinths. At first glance, they looked like delicately carved ivory figures or bizarre porcelain effigies. In fact, I discovered, they were "airport art" bought at a local import house and lacquered white by the designer himself. Sofas were upholstered in white Naugahyde bound with expensive wool cord tied as carelessly as twine. He loved this paradox, which Andree Putman dubbed "rich and poor."And there were always blueprints and drawings push-pinned to the walls, maybe a new prototype, fabric swatches, gifts in Tiffany boxes, books and magazines to intrigue the visitor. ¶ In John's realm, under the gaze of two enormous fiberglass phrenology heads, you were on stage and wanted to be your best. I'd approach the piano very slowly so that John would keep playing. The moment was magic, and we'd start a

In John Dickinson's firehouse bedroom stands a 15-foot-high four-poster of hand-carved *faux* bamboo with a black fitted cover. Redwood wainscotting was stripped and given coats of varnish to emphasize the grain, and to give the nostalgic air of an old railroad station waiting room, said the designer. Walls are covered in horsehair-textured black vinyl. Double french doors open to a sheltered balcony overlooking a brick-paved garden, its symmetry emphasized by neat squares of clipped boxwood bushes.

morning of interviewing and reviewing in an up-tempo mood. ❡ Other Sundays, John would hold court in his magnificent four-poster bed—hand-carved and painted to look like bamboo, and covered with a black woven cashmere throw. The walls of his bedroom were black "horsehair," offset with redwood wainscotting and a pair of hand-painted chests. ❡ John was opinionated, witty, and very down-to-earth. "Prettiness has nothing to do with style," he said. "If you're stripping down rooms and editing, as I do, there's no place for it. Logic precludes prettiness." "A color scheme is a questionable device on which to base a room's design," he noted. ❡ John Dickinson died in 1982, and the book project was set aside. When I took it up again, I decided to expand its scope and make it a tribute to all the designers of San Francisco. ❡ I asked John Vaughan, the brightest and best young photographer of interiors, to join me on the project. We ran through all our lists and photographs, reviewed hundreds of houses and apartments, and with great care chose our favorites. Not for one moment did we plan a scientifically mapped tome that included every architect, designer, or hill. Still, the finest work is represented here. We've covered the City and places City people escape to on weekends. ❡ After reading these pages, you'll have a sense of wonderful lives lived to the fullest in remarkable settings. Passions of San Franciscans— from art collections and art deco furniture to gardens and pets—are all here. Perhaps most exciting and revealing is the design talent we discovered on film. Gary Hutton's synthesis of Victoriana with today's simplicity, Michael Taylor's grandeur, Jan Dutton's ethereal laces, and Ami Magill's murals in Diane Burn's nursery are a revelation. ❡ Robert Hutchinson's sculpted walls are his setting for Indian baskets, clay bowls, European paintings, and an extraordinary orchid collection. ❡ John and Dodie Rosekrans were two of Michael Taylor's best clients, and their interiors reflect that ideal collaboration between informed, curious clients and their designer. Standing on a bluff overlooking the San Francisco Bay, their house would be remarkable anywhere. ❡ These pages also reveal worldliness and a preference for comfort over pompousness or pretension. These rooms were not designed to speed the owners' way up the social ladder, to suggest centuries of ancestors, or to affix the designer's name forever to the furniture. ❡ Anthony Hail's refined rooms could be in London or Paris, but most interiors on these pages could exist only here. Quintessentially Californian, Ron Mann's designs seem to spring from the earth. Using massive Douglas fir slabs, cast stone, sand-cast bronze, wrought iron, and very direct forms, he creates designs and rooms that are at once surprising and very comforting in their sophistication and simplicity. The pages of this book celebrate this search for individuality. ❡ Just as John Dickinson taught me to see design from a new perspective, I want these pages to give a new view of San Francisco. Behind the closed doors and curtained windows are some glorious rooms.

Diane Dorrans Saeks
San Francisco, June, 1989

Opposite: **Ron Mann's vibrant interior designs are fully realized, comfortable rooms. Here in a Montara oceanside house, a no-color, no-pattern bedroom scheme gains drama from overscale furniture, a floor of recycled douglas fir planks with concrete grouting, and Mann's sure-footed multi-level floor plan. Firewood stacked outside the window stays as summer sculpture. Angleback wicker chairs designed by Ivy Rosequist for Wicker Wicker Wicker. Papier-mâché whale sculpture by Steven Mann.**

Grand Style

An occasional minor earthquake or rumbling temblor shakes the calm of the City and reminds residents of a more precarious time when an earthquake and fire destroyed its heart. Otherwise, San Francisco seems to have been standing on these hills forever—or at least longer than a mere 140 years or so. ❡ Grand mansions and patrician palazzi edging the bluffs of Pacific Heights and circling Lafayette Park give the distinct impression that they set up residence centuries ago. Solid fortunes made from sugar, gold, railroads, and real-estate speculation provided these grandstand positions, their proud profiles, and the classic Mediterranean-and European-influenced architecture. ❡ In fact, in 1776, the San Francisco Bay that greeted Lieutenant Colonel Juan Bautista de Anza and his band of Spanish settlers was sandy, wind-swept, and wild, with few trees to provide shelter. The rocky hills and headlands beyond the north tower of the Golden Gate Bridge today give some idea of the terrain. Few new settlers arrived on this hardship post in the 60 years following the establishment of the Presidio and the mission. ❡ Around 1835, an Englishman, William A. Richardson, built a house in what is now Portsmouth Square, and the village of Yerba Buena began. A straggly collection of pueblos, huts, tents, and tacked-together shacks huddled around a cove and provided shelter for those first San Franciscans. California was proclaimed part of the United States by treaty in 1846, and soon the land to the north and south of Market Street was surveyed, and rough streets and paths crisscrossed the hills. Fortune seekers arrived. The Gold Rush was on. ❡ City lots in those days may have been sold for as little as $90. But with later speculation, an acre could increase in value from $500 to $20,000 in just a decade. ❡ In the 1850s and 1860s, the fanciest part of town was Rincon Hill. Andrew Hallidie's invention, the cable car, tamed steep Nob Hill in 1873 and gave instant status to the area. As more lines were added, Russian Hill became a desirable address. ❡ In the years between 1870 and 1906, as the City boomed, thousands of houses, most of them Victorian-style, were built. San Francisco extended west from grand Nob Hill, east from South Park, and south beyond the Mission. Grand boulevards like Van Ness Avenue and Dolores Avenue were lined with impressive mansions. Handsome houses in well-tended gardens stood in solitary splendor in Pacific Heights with grand vistas of the Bay.

After extensive refurbishing directed by interior designer Anthony Hail, the main residence of Filoli is now open to the public for viewing. To recreate the interiors as they looked in the twenties, Hail gathered together furniture and paintings bequeathed by Lurline Roth, one of the estate's residents, and special pieces loaned from the Getty Museum, the California Palace of the Legion of Honor, and the M.H. de Young Memorial Museum. *Previous pages:* The ballroom at Filoli with murals painted in 1925 by Ernest Peixotto, a well-known illustrator. The chandelier was said to once hang in the Hall of Mirrors at Versailles. Crystal sconces have amethyst drops.
Opposite: The refurbished Filoli dining room has Chippendale-style chairs and an eighteenth-century Dutch cabinet. Filoli, a half-hour drive south of San Francisco, may be visited by advance reservation (415-364-2880).

Then came the Great Earthquake and Fire and the end of ostentatious turreted castles, mansions, and fanciful chalets on Nob Hill and Russian Hill. The grandes dames on the heights were spared, and the trauma was soon over. Spirits revived, and after briefly sheltering in Golden Gate Park, residents returned and rebuilt, this time with fire-proof steel frames. ¶ Undaunted by the thought of another quake (even today, few people really worry about fault-lines or tremors), San Franciscans swiftly built *beaux arts* mansions, neo-classical manor houses, Dutch Colonial mansions, grandly curlicued apartment buildings, and handsome Spanish Colonial Revival-style dwellings to house the wealthy and would-be's alike. ¶ Walking tours along outer Broadway, up and down Pierce and Steiner, Vallejo and Green streets, around Alta Plaza and the Presidio Wall show many turn-of-the-century mansions still occupying favored status. There are houses by Willis Polk—even a beauty built by Joseph Strauss, the structural engineer for the Golden Gate Bridge. The mild weather in San Francisco is kind to their splendor; owners care for them diligently and trim the pretty topiaries and evergreen trees. ¶ Not surprisingly, San Francisco's mansions are now million-dollar babies. No doubt their original go-getter owners would be very pleased.

Filoli's French Room has elaborate French chairs upholstered with Aubusson tapestries, on Aubusson carpets. Flowers from the Filoli gardens fill the rooms, which were designed for entertainment on a grand scale. (Fans of "Dynasty" may recognize Filoli. The television series' pilot was filmed there, and stock footage of the 654-acre property occasionally appears.)

FILOLI, WOODSIDE

Many of California's top architects and designers have worked on the buildings and interiors of Filoli. Willis Polk desgined the 43-room house. The highly acclaimed gardens were originally designed by Isabella Worn.

We can thank Mr. and Mrs. William Bowers Bourn II, San Francisco architect Willis Polk, and an enormous fortune gained from gold and spring water for Filoli, the elegant 654-acre estate 30 miles south of San Francisco. Named for a credo admired by owner Bourn—FIght for a just cause, LOve your fellow man, LIve a good life—Filoli was built between 1915 and 1917 and offers glimpses of California life on a grand scale. ¶ Polk had designed the Bourn's brick townhouse (still standing on Webster Street, between Broadway and Pacific Avenue) and in 1915 began work on their Woodside country estate. ¶ On watershed lands to the south of Crystal Lake, he sited the mansion among a magnificent stand of live oak trees. Bruce Porter, known for his stained-glass windows and murals, planned the Italian/French-style gardens, which were planted by Isabella Worn. ¶ The exteriors of the house are often called modified Georgian in style, but the inventive Polk brought together several other architectural traditions. The interiors are primarily English-and French-influenced, while the tile roof is in the Spanish tradition. ¶ The interiors contain 43 rooms and a total of about 43,000 square feet, including servants'

For many years, Filoli has been known for its superbly planted gardens, but the residence stood empty. First-floor rooms, including the French room, the ballroom, and library, are now furnished as they were when the Bourn family were residents. The Filoli estate is 30 miles south of San Francisco.

quarters and a ballroom. ¶ Long, wide hallways provide easy circulation to all rooms. Beautifully proportioned rooms with 17-foot ceilings, glorious wood-panelled walls, wood-burning fireplaces, and lovely views of the gardens from the windows create visions of a grand California country life. ¶ The massive ormolu-decorated fireplace and magnificent murals in the ballroom depicting the Lakes of Killarney and the Bourn's Irish estate are of particular interest. A study of the floors throughout the first floor reveals acacia koa wood in the study, quarter-sawn oak parquetry in the grand ballroom, and walnut laid in a herringbone design in the library. ¶ After a tour of the house, visitors can spend hours walking through the Walled Garden, the Sunken Garden, the Rose Garden, the Yew Allee, with its espaliered apple and pear trees, and the Woodland Garden with its marble plaque, inscribed *Festina Lente* (Make Haste Slowly), an excellent motto for enjoying Filoli and its gardens. ¶ The gardens and interiors of Filoli are open to the public between February and November by advance reservation. Filoli is a property of the National Trust for Historic Preservation in the United States. Telephone (415) 364-2880 for information and reservations.

ROSEKRANS HOUSE, PACIFIC HEIGHTS

A quartet of opulent gilded armchairs stands in the extraordinary Rosekrans living room. California-born designer Michael Taylor had a remarkable understanding of furniture scale and placement. He planned a large, comfortable sofa, a seemingly artless juxtaposition of refined and earthy materials, plus chairs to cluster for party conversations. From the arched windows, views across the Bay to the Marin Headlands. Bronze figure by Italian sculptor Emilio Greco.

Early in the century, when ornate High-Victorian architecture was in full bloom in San Francisco, Mr. and Mrs. Andrew Welch had the wit and imagination to hire architect/classicist Willis Jefferson Polk to design their new Pacific Heights mansion.

¶ For inspiration, the cosmopolitan couple and the worldly Polk turned to a Spanish Renaissance palace, the lyrical Casa de Zaporta in Saragossa. As in Spain, the exterior is understated, the interior quite theatrical and grand. Entry to the 1917 mansion is through a dramatic two-story atrium, intricately carved with sandstone columns, balconies, and friezes, all closely replicating the original.

¶ After Mrs. Welch willed the mansion to the archdiocese of San Francisco, it was beautifully maintained as the Archbishop's Palace for 40 years. ¶ When John and Dodie Rosekrans bought the house in 1979, they covered the soaring atrium with a greenhouse roof to halt erosion of the sandstone carvings and to provide a year-round room for entertaining. Giant palms enhance this exotic courtyard.

¶ The couple brought in a friend, interior designer Michael Taylor, to furnish the grand rooms. Choosing chairs, tables, and sofas and art of character and bold scale, Taylor has

imbued the mansion with style and comfort. Here, as in his favorite clients' houses, the designer is at his best, creating rooms of cosmopolitan charm and eclectic individuality far from the pared-down "California Look" he helped popularize. ❡ Here, an eighteenth-century Samarkand rug provides a geometric counterpoint to a quartet of gilded armchairs. A contemporary Italian sculpture is juxtaposed with an extraordinary 12-panel coromandel screen. African village sculpture stands beside contemporary California sculpture. ❡ "While a room should be beautiful, it should not be too perfect," said Taylor. "Perfection in every detail usually makes a room studied, formal, rather dull, and even forbidding." ❡ The set of four over-scale, scroll-armed, gilded armchairs (just one is an eighteenth-century original) were upholstered in rich golden silk. Eight straight-backed English hall chairs are placed around a new travertine-topped dining table, Taylor's own design. ❡ In the smoking room, walls are covered in pale-gold grass cloth, a subtle backdrop for the extraordinary collection of sculptures, quartz crystals, carvings, and plants. The room is also a show-case for a Senufo bird carving and prehistoric stone objects on a travertine table.

From the open-air terrace of this Willis Polk house, visitors can enjoy a view of two other wonders of San Francisco—the Palace of Fine Arts, *above,* originally designed by Polk's teacher, Bernard Maybeck, and the Golden Gate Bridge. In the superbly proportioned bedroom, with intricately carved pilasters, the draped Majorcan bed is as beautifully finished as a couture gown.

California design at its cosmopolitan best, *opposite,* in the Rosekrans bedroom. The atrium/entry was faithfully modeled after a courtyard of a Spanish Renaissance palace, the Casa de Zaporta in Saragossa. *Left:* urns and busts displayed before the fine view.

In the quietness and luxe of interior designer Anthony Hail's Russian Hill sitting room, it would be easy to imagine that he lives somewhere in Belgravia or in a very chic Paris *arrondissement* overlooking a private park. San Francisco rush hour may be in full throttle, but Hail's rooms offer few clues of a bustling city outside. ❡ Along the enfilade of his rooms, through lacquered double doors, are glimpses of museum-quality antiques, seventeenth-century Esfahan carpets, with impressionist light filtering through the windows. The house, a Victorian first renovated by architect Julia Morgan in 1916, was completely remodeled by Hail to improve the rooms' proportions. ❡ "Soon after we moved into this house, I realized that I didn't have one stick of furniture, not one decorative object, that is new. Actually my taste runs to furniture of the late eighteenth century. I don't seem to keep anything later than 1800. Maybe I should appreciate modern things more," mused the handsome Hail, a Tennessee native who started collecting antiques right out of Harvard. ❡ His taste runs to the classical, the refined, the subtle. And while anything Louis XVI (*late Louis Seize*) is automatically a favorite, he's

The house owned by Anthony Hail and his business partner, Charles Posey, stands on one of the few flat blocks of Russian Hill. From a small, elegant entry, stairs lead to the sitting room, which has windows on three sides.

One of Anthony Hail's heroines is Edith Wharton, whose opinionated 1897 book, *The Decoration of Houses,* is often seen as the coming of age of American architecture and the beginning of interior design as we know it today. She would certainly approve of the balance, symmetry, appropriateness, and luxury of Hail's house.

also very partial to low-key Northern European antiques. In his bedroom sits a Danish Louis XVI mechanical architect's table, one of his favorite pieces. ❡ "Living and working with antiques is my whole life, the main focus of everything I do," said Hail, a fixture of the San Francisco decorating and social scene since he arrived from New York in 1955. ❡ Still, Hail is no great respecter of borders. With his acquisitions, he brings to his rooms French chairs, Chinese lacquer tables, English bookcases, Russian chandeliers, Swedish prints, and Persian rugs, mixed with American know-how.

Hail's striped bedroom, *opposite,* displays the luxury of beautiful light, and his thoughtful placement of favorite drawings and furniture. *Below:* a gentleman's bathroom.

"I see each room as a lifetime proposition. The way I work is never instant decorating. First, and most important, I do as much as I can to get the architecture right, to make a wonderful background for antiques and people. Then I find a few beautiful antiques—rugs, vases, lamp bases, bookcases," said Hail, explaining his approach. ❧ "I find I am working with fewer antiques than I used to. No one can afford a whole room of antiques any more. The point is that you can start with antiques from your family and add to them over the years. Reproductions can be very beautiful. I line them all and have them smell quite wonderful. And I usually do plain curtains—that way you don't get tired of looking at them, and they don't overpower the room," he said. ❧ "I always remind my clients, 'Remember, this is not a museum you're creating.' You must have table tops that can take drinks, plus sturdy chairs that men can sit in. Fabrics must wear well, and not be so precious that friends are afraid to relax," said the pragmatic Hail. ❧ "None of my own house is just for display, and I insist that clients use all of their rooms. You must live with your antiques. I sit in these chairs. I bring out my best china every day." ❧ Don't Spare the Horses is his motto. "Beauty and pleasure are givens, but rooms must be usable, not fragile or intimidating, "Hail said.

In Hillsborough—a fast 30-minute drive south into the Peninsula—stands one of the most remarkable residences in California. Built 20 years ago of stone quarried in Sonoma County, the house is the result of a collaboration between owners George and Elaine McKeon, architect Angus MacSweeny, and interior designer Michael Taylor. ¶ MacSweeney drew up the original plans. When he died midway into the project, the McKeons hired interior designer Michael Taylor at the suggestion of their friend Dodie Rosekrans (see page 31). ¶ It was Taylor who designed the extraordinary oak-beamed ceiling in the living room and stained it a pale sand-beige. Over five years, he added over-scale sofas upholstered in linen velvet and an extraordinary collection of furnishings and antiques. ¶ "Michael thought the finest furniture was created in the eighteenth century, so we found French, English, Chinese, and Venetian pieces from that period. He's known for inspiring the "California Look," but he used antiques with great flair. They had to be the finest quality and unusual," said Elaine McKeon, president of the board of trustees, San Francisco Museum of Modern Art.

Michael Taylor would walk into this 52' x 26' living room and tell the owner it was the most comfortable room he had ever designed. The oak panelling formerly graced the Great Hall of Moreton Paddocks, Warwickshire, England. A rare George I (ca. 1720) cabriole-legged stool of walnut and parcel gilt with a silk seat stands in the center of the grand room.

A pair of Queen Anne mirrors hangs above Taylor-designed "rock pile" console tables. Oak shutters with a "linen-fold" design were distressed to appear old.

For her remarkable five-acre property with its 67 California oaks, Elaine McKeon first hired landscape architect Thomas Church to design and plan the landscape. He laid out the patios, pool, and shady loggia, and had all the trees (including stone pines) trimmed. After Church died, landscape architect Garrett Eckbo completed and revised the garden. Every March, gardeners plant 50 flats of impatiens around the giant California live oaks. In the sunny Peninsula climate, the flowers flourish until November. Classic roses like Peace, Queen Elizabeth, First Prize, and Tropicana are among McKeon's favorites. *Opposite:* Teak furniture invites year-round gatherings of family and friends.

Oak panelling in the entrance
hall was formerly at home in the
Old Rectory, Amersham,
Buckinghamshire. Taylor's keen
eye discovered an English
console table in the manner of
William Kent (1760) and topped
it with an elaborately carved
gilt-wood George II mirror.
In the center of the marble-tiled
hall is a fine Elizabethan oak
refectory table (ca.1590).

The Designers

San Francisco has been blessed with a remarkably talented group of interior designers who find their inspiration in the gracious beauty of the region and around the world. They're highly individual and experimental, pulling out all stops for both adventurous and old-line clients. ¶ In a city where almost everyone comes from "somewhere else," no single look, trend, or style predominates. Some designers have made an art of strict minimalism, while others call on a fine band of local craftsmen to lacquer, incise, *faux* paint, sew, and stencil their designs to a fare-thee-well. ¶ Certainly, traditional rooms are most popular, but in young California it's hard to take period rooms too seriously. So designers mix countries-of-origin and periods, create instant heirlooms, juxtapose fine and folk antiques, contrast new materials with ancient stones and minerals. In rooms with good bones, thanks to exemplary architecture, they hang California artists' paintings and showcase contemporary crafts. They design comfortable viewing pavilions for glorious vistas. And they fashion urbane rooms illuminated with San Francisco's clear light and warmed by the California sun. ¶ For certain clients, designers may offer opulence, but as John Dickinson noted, a designer's life is not all deluxe. "Tacky things with grand things, mundane with exotic things give rooms vitality," he said. Dickinson also loved novelty in his rooms, but noted that a room based on amusing ideas would not be a laugh. ¶ San Francisco's designers revere the past and design's finest moments, but history does not weigh heavily on their shoulders. It's a rare house that was built before the turn of the century—the twentieth century. Designers in San Francisco can start anew each day. ¶ "When I've got my creativity going, that's when I'm most alive and conscious. When I'm solving design problems, rethinking an old design, I really feel life around me," said designer Ron Mann, who credits nature as his true source of inspiration. ¶ Designers use Chinese and Japanese antiques in a contemporary setting, happily work with luscious silks and romantic chintzes, as well as plain cotton canvas. Lighthearted, sun-struck colors wear well when the temperature seldom dips below 50 degrees or soars to 75 degrees. Never concerned with providing respite from a harsh climate, designers have carte blanche to dream. ¶ Labels and pretension don't belong here. Rather, each designer goes his or her own way, reinventing as they go along.

In John Dickinson's Victorian firehouse, the sky-lit ceiling and walls are as the designer found them, a mottled topaz. In the hallway, a dresser of *faux ivoire* handpainted by Dickinson. An imposing pair of heads between shuttered windows was acquired from a sale at the Old Spaghetti Factory (a former North Beach landmark) and refinished. *Overleaf:* Dickinson creates his own room patterns with a highly disciplined no-color scheme that emphasizes the outlines of the plaster tables and curvy Victorian chairs in changing light from the south-facing windows. The pair of paintings is by Ralph Du Casse (see his house on page 172).

The highly recognizable "California Look"—paled-down creamy colors and haute-casual overstuffed upholstery in light-filled rooms accessorized with elements of nature—is beloved in a city that likes barefoot ease presented with sophistication. ❡ Design stars like Michael Taylor (originally from Modesto) and the late John Dickinson (raised in Berkeley) have become admired internationally. Both have profoundly influenced today's designers. Missouri-born Mann has a free-spirited approach that encourages his followers to bring nature indoors—to use timbers, stone, and weather-worn rocks as part of a highly polished interior. ❡ Chuck Winslow, originally from the East Coast, likes to juxtapose contemporary art and an international cast of antique furniture. "The combination can be a marvelous visual surprise. Looking for the less obvious combination is the key," said Winslow. ❡ Performing their own neat balancing act on the edge of the Pacific Ocean, San Francisco's designers introduce the world to new possibilities.

An 1893 firehouse with brass name plates and a white canvas-curtained portiere was the remarkable residence and office for designer John Dickinson for 15 years until he died in 1982. ❡ Certainly the finest example of his work, it was also his design laboratory. There was magic, elegance, and mystery in his rooms. Where fire engines once stood, Dickinson parked his black-lacquered vintage Jaguar, its flanks ornamented with natural woven cane. Guests walked up a narrow flight of redwood stairs, worn by the boots of firemen and his many friends to a gray patina. At the top, an oversized white-enamelled door swung open to reveal one enormous sky-lit room (formerly the firemen's dormitory) that served John both as living room and studio. ❡ Dickinson said, "The walls are just as I found them—cracked old plaster, but the color of smoky topaz. I had them washed and touched up a bit, and painted the old dado white. The partitioning walls for the new kitchen and dressing room are new, but look old, thanks to a great *trompe l'oeil* job by Carole Lansdown." ❡ "The fireplace took a year to execute," recalled Dickinson. "It's nickel-plated steel and brass with moldings that match the dados. They're both the same distance from the floor, a fine point no one cares about but me." ❡ Later would come John's plaster tables, white

Standing on two white-lacquered plinths and displayed in an oak cabinet were John's attenuated white-lacquered carved African figures, a brilliant use of "airport art." To infer that he bought them en route to Mombasa or Zanzibar would be romantic. In fact, John gathered the collection at Cost Plus for a few dollars but spent considerably more getting the finest lacquer job.

Naugahyde-upholstered sofas, ten Victorian chairs upholstered in taupe leather and piped in white, an art nouveau table of grand proportions, plus a pair of carnival heads on columns that also housed speakers and storage. ¶ Just before John died, his last table made its appearance alongside his sofas. It was a design that pleased him very much—a wood table carved and lacquered to look like a cube with a bulky horse blanket thrown over it. The table's solid shape, he said, would be just right in a room where there were already enough furniture legs. ¶ In all his work, designer John Dickinson was unintentionally a trend-setter. Using menswear tweeds, camelhair, and gray flannels for upholstery, wall-coverings, and luxurious lap robes had his imprimatur first. Plain, honest materials—like unbleached canvas, woven wools, unstained wood, leather with piping, gray industrial carpet—were enhanced by the gleam of steel and brass and lots of sparkling white paint. And often he introduced something a little unsettling—carved or real bleached bones, a pencil drawing of a skull, bird claws. "Taste is a word I avoid," he once said. "'Good' or 'bad,' it's all so nebulous. The more you're dealing solely with taste in a room, the more you're on shaky ground. Give me vulgarity any time. I find it has great vitality."

Accessories that made walk-on appearances in John Dickinson's firehouse at various times included a shell basket filled with white conch shells; architectural models; an African tribal stool and headrests; Italian alabaster fruit; ceramic phrenology heads; a white bowl of onyx eggs; a flat, white stoneware dish of perfectly oval gray river stones; a collection of crystal and brass eggs, bleached coral branches, ship sextants, brass firehose nozzles, carved fruitwood bones, along with his standard white ironware ashtrays and stacks of books. Still, his rooms were clearly not about mere styling. "I don't put my stamp on a room by styling—doing things like plumping cushions with a knife-chop or fluffing up the curtains. Then design becomes ephemeral," Dickinson said. "Basic construction of a room should be where good design comes from; otherwise, it is not really style."

CHARLES PFISTER APARTMENT, NOB HILL

Full-height casement windows fill the rooms with light. Classic canvas-covered sofas and chairs in the salon were designed by Charles Pfister for Knoll and make the perfect accompaniment to his gilded *fauteuils,* granite-topped tripod tables, and extraordinary plants.

I think the location of my apartment, right at the summit of Nob Hill, is nonpareil. It overlooks Huntington Park and the historic Pacific Union Club. And the exterior and interior of the 1927 building have a great sense of proportion and scale. I find it just as glamorous and urbane as could be," said architect/designer Charles Pfister, whose clients nevertheless often call him away to London, Tokyo, The Hague, and New York. ¶ "I've lived here for five years, and the furnishings are still changing. Things come and go, and I don't think of it as 'finished.' I know I'll add more treasures, or retire an old favorite. This is the way it is now but not necessarily forever." ¶ When he first moved into these grand rooms, Pfister opted for a paled-down background. Mirrors on the walls further enlarge the apparent size of his rooms. Restoring his apartment in the spirit, style, and character of the original, he saw no reason to alter the interior architecture. ¶ Diffused northern light emphasizes the appealing pallor of the rooms.

The only real color in these powder-pale rooms comes from a handsome early nineteenth-century French needlepoint rug in the salon. Pfister had his Thonet deco dining chairs (bought at auction from the historic old Palace Hotel) finished in a subtle bronze lacquer. Floors were deliberately left bare.

Night and day create very different moods here. Early morning sun fills the rooms with cheer and brightly illuminates every crisp corner. Nighttime, with lights dimmed, the space expands, and Hutton's setting is as glamorous as a thirties private club.

A friend of mine said my studio reminded him of a dentist's office in Los Angeles in the fifties," said interior designer Gary Hutton. His Mission District apartment/ studio is located in a one-story building built for light industry in 1946. Still, with its exposed concrete walls, concrete floor, steel-framed wrap-around windows, exposed-beam ceilings, and clean lines, it was the perfect setting for Hutton. He had been looking for a building where he could set up office and use the rooms as a lab for new designs. ¶ Patterns of sunlight streak through the apartment— actually one large room with an office, a kitchen, and a new sky-lit bathroom. ¶ Walls were painted white, the floor sealed and stained black. Metal shades on the high windows look forties period-perfect, but they're actually new. "I wanted to keep the design fresh and crisp with lots of texture. The scheme had to make sense with the architecture and its period. Chintz wouldn't exactly do it," said the designer. ¶ He set up a dining/ conference room in one sunny corner, a comfortable sitting room with high-backed linen-upholstered sofas in another corner. ¶ A pair of geometric-patterned thirties Turkish rugs, found by chance in an antique store, look as if they were recently designed by Hutton himself.

In the sitting area are three cigarette tables that look like antique bronzes. They were designed by Gary Hutton using a lacquered gold-leaf finish on fiberglass. "It's a complicated and extravagant finish, but I had to mute the gold effect because it's too luxe for an industrial building," said Hutton. While he keeps accessories and *objets* to a carefully edited minimum, Hutton continues to add turn-of-the-century Rookwood pottery, paintings of rural scenes by American artists, and handcrafted glass. In fact, nothing in this scheme is set forever, as Hutton continues to experiment, observe, learn, and design. New chairs and tables will doubtless come and go, making brief appearances before moving on to clients and friends. With the black-and-white scheme, open plan, and Hutton's endless appreciation of the classic and the new, the studio will soon look completely different. Hutton's stylish apartment owes everything to his go-for-it approach and nothing to the once-historic-but-now-changing neighborhood. Always experimenting, Hutton plays with scale, new materials, different furniture arrangements, and lighting.

TEDRICK AND BENNETT COTTAGE, RUSSIAN HILL

The French military scene on the nine-foot screen along one wall of their living room presents a diverting tableau. "Our French screen gives the room dimension and an extra 'outdoor' view, a different window on the world," said designer Michael Tedrick. He and Tom Bennett are also fond of natural-fiber textiles in subtle, faded colors. Here, they've chosen a luxurious woven raw silk for simple curtains, plus nubby tweeds and long-staple cotton for upholstery, throws, and pillows. Passionate collectors, the two have gathered diverse but harmonious antiques.

A tiny, charming cottage is not exactly what you expect to find on grand Russian Hill, but tucked away in quiet lanes and along zigzag pathways are some of the City's most prized locations. ¶ A few years ago, interior design partners Michael Tedrick and Thomas Bennett were lucky enough to discover this sunny two-bedroom cottage. Its sheltered brick-paved garden terrace, bay views, and privacy add to its cachet. The cottage is part of a William Wurster-designed complex built in the thirties. ¶ Tedrick and Bennett have used the rooms as their laboratory, ignoring formula decorating in favor of their own mix of international antiques, muted colors, and textural fabrics. Their seemingly artless approach brings together a striking eight-panel Napoleonic wallpaper screen, a Directoire chest of drawers, a pair of Welsh jockey benches, a French zinc table with a Brazilian blue-granite top, plus new pine tables by Tony Cowan of Cottage Tables. Quirky Japanese antique fabrics, baskets, and pottery bring their own character. ¶ "We like to be surrounded with the things we love," they said. "We appreciate the hands-on craft and inherent beauty of each piece." ¶ Still, their interests range widely, and their rooms evolve slowly and thoughtfully. Chances are, in a few years, this same view will be completely different.

In a famous Nob Hill apartment building (ca. 1912), Jois Belfield worked with her favorite palette. Her rooms have a feeling of pared-down luxury with rich silks, textured linens, a white wool carpet, handpainted bronze canvas, and natural canvas.

The elaborate moldings in her four-bedroom apartment reminded designer Jois Belfield of an iced wedding cake. ❡ "I painted the walls a 'clotted cream' color so that they wouldn't look too stuffy. It's a more interesting tone than pure white because it changes with the season and the time of day. In the morning, the rooms look crisp. In afternoon light, the 'thick cream' color looks pale golden. There's something about the light in San Francisco that makes this exact tone work wonderfully," she said. ❡ For contrast, Belfield chose bronze tables and the dash of pink silk on pillows. ❡ So that the living room wouldn't look too "sweet" or "prissy," she stacked oak firewood next to the fireplace. "The room needs that roughness," said Belfield.

"In a building of this grand style and age, you'd expect silk draperies on the windows. Instead, I did plain white canvas draped casually," she said.

In this 1906 cottage, museum-caliber antiques live happily with contemporary classics like architect Warren Platner's wire-rod tables. ¶ Interior designer Chuck Winslow is a master at creating pretty rooms with character, comfort, and vitality. In his design schemes, neoclassical chairs, Chinese antiques, romantic chintzes, provocative contemporary paintings, imaginative tabletop collections, humble cottons, extravagant silks and gilding, fine craftmanship, and comfortable-as-an-old-shoe furniture come together in rooms of great charm and authority. ¶ "My dream decorating has a look that's all very offhand," said the designer, "but, of course, it takes attention to detail, scale, and quality to make that work." ¶ There's a reverence for the past, but it's given snap with offbeat colors and contemporary art. Nothing "matches" in the conventional sense, but everything works together to

All rooms in Chuck Winslow's cottage work hard. "My rooms change from day to day, season to season," said the designer. *Above:* pine bookshelves frame the marble fireplace surround. Pink walls, pink pigskin suede, a fat sofa upholstered in linen, and sisal carpet create a gentle, relaxed mood. *Opposite:* a painting by Delia Doherty in the entry hall.

In the salon, crystal candlesticks, Warren Platner's sixties wire-rod tables, an antique dhurrie, and Italian chairs with turquoise pillows. Dog-lover Winslow also displays his growing collection of *papier-mâché* and folk art hounds.

create a room you've never seen before. The designer adds the backbone of East Coast formality to informal, California-cool country houses, and his irreverence for grandeur to urbane apartments. ¶ "Rooms should always look as if they happened over years, updated spontaneously with new paintings and unusual furniture," said Winslow. "They should show signs of life, echoes of human voices, and hands-on history. ¶ The designer uses tabletops and walls as his canvas, composing eye-pleasing tablescapes with favorite sculptures, small-scale paintings, glorious flowers, crystal candlesticks, and stacks of art books. Still, his rooms never feel cluttered. ¶ "I move things around all the time. Nothing stays in the same place for very long; otherwise, you lose the joy and surprise of seeing it," said Winslow.

Chic California comfort thrives under the sure hand of interior designer William Whiteside in his studio apartment overlooking Alta Plaza. Luxurious materials—glove leather, raw silk—and a well-edited collection of art and objects provide pleasures for the hand and the eye. The sisal carpet was a practical, low-key choice. ❡ The imposing scale of the Italianate mantelpiece and a Japanese *tansu* (chest), and three overstuffed, leather-covered chairs and ottomans all seem to amplify the studio space. ❡ Throughout, Whiteside combined rugged textures and rough surfaces to rein in the opulence. His deft mix of East and West— Chinese chairs, the hefty and highly detailed *tansu*, classic moldings, exotic flowers, and soothing colors—is often a feature of San Francisco interiors.

In William Whiteside's beautifully appointed sunny studio, three Japanese millstones are displayed on the massive mantel. Fat down-filled club chairs and cushy ottomans provide a versatile seating plan for fireside suppers, early morning newspaper reading, and foggy-day musing. The studio is on the first floor of a shingled townhouse designed by Willis Polk.

Starting with a very umpromising block-walled sky-lit loft short on architectural interest and free of interior walls, designer Ron Mann created a studio of dramatic simplicity. Furnished with his own furniture and accessories, the loft changes with the season and the designer's whim, with new items making their appearance as they roll from his drawing board. ¶ "I've now come to a place in my life where I'm living out my design fantasies," said Mann, whose métier is usually a natural material like weathered wood, pale stone, verdigris'd bronze, undyed canvas or white plaster in a paled-down color scheme. ¶ "The open space of this studio gave me such a wonderful freedom to experiment and try new ideas. I've painted the floor, added platforms to delineate a sitting area and an office. Since I've always got new designs brewing, it's a wonderful way to test

To warm up a concrete floor, Missouri-born Ron Mann handpainted and tooled this instant white "rug." Curvy cotton-duck upholstered sofa, and stone chest of drawers are his own designs. Chair from Wicker Wicker Wicker.

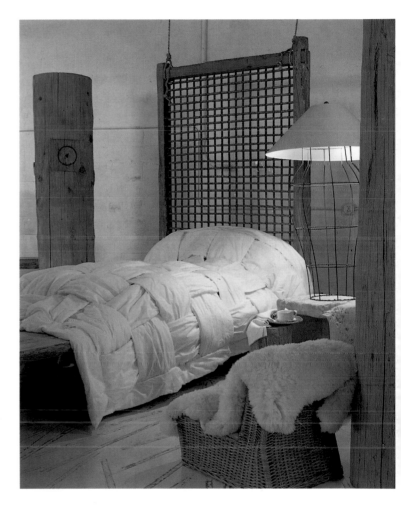

Designer Ron Mann's bold new quilt, artfully crafted in woven strips of pure white padded cotton, drapes his new sleeping platform. "Headboard" is an antique Majorcan screen. Wicker chair by Ivy Rosequist.

them, look at them in all possible lights, try them on for size, and get to know them," he said. ¶ There's real comfort, sensuality, and rough-hewn charm in his designs, with none of the trappings and pretensions that often accompany today's interiors. He pays homage to the rocks and noble timbers of California with his tables, lamps, and chairs, but this is no simple-minded, back-to-nature love affair. ¶ The Mendocino and Big Sur coasts offer up driftwood logs, and Mann's travels to Majorca and Mexico yield new designs of sophistication and grace prized by cognoscenti around the world.

Ron Mann loves to surround himself with his newest designs. Here, a Spring roomscape includes a Portuguese cupboard filled with variations of his sandcast bronze shadow vases and plates. Cor-Ten steel candleholders on the driftwood table are also his designs.

In Craig Leavitt and Stephen Weaver's Russian Hill apartment, it's very much Louis-meets-Leavitt-and-Weaver. This talented pair of designers nonchalantly mixed fine French furniture, New Guinea wood carvings, a Parisian park chair, their own over-scale "Javelin" lamps with huge parchment shades, and an eclectic collection of luxurious fabrics. Needlepoint pillows (stitched with aphorisms by a friend with a tart tongue) and rich memorabilia are counterpoints in the monochromatic scheme. ¶ These elegant, witty rooms, with their pale northern light, are proof positive that designers often do their best work for themselves with no client running interference. ¶ "We like to let the rooms happen rather than work with a floor plan," said Weaver. "In a sense, we don't make a big effort. We love rooms that look a little worn. Fading and wear give rooms a reso-nance and comfort we like." ¶ Tone-on-tone textured plaster walls, luxurious wool fabrics, and leather upholstery offer tactile pleasures. ¶ "If the design of accessories and furniture is top-quality," said Leavitt, "it will all work. We like simple proportions with rich details." ¶ "We edit carefully. We're always tempted to gather all our favorite things around us," noted Weaver.

Craig Leavitt and Stephen Weaver mix their own dramatic furniture designs with favorite antiques. In the living room of their Russian Hill apartment, Weaver's painting of Leavitt's 12 favorite rooms hangs on a raked plaster wall. "Arrowhead" granite-topped table and "Javelin" lamp are their own designs, *opposite.* The designers brought together a suede-upholstered Italian chair, a New Guinea story-board carving, and their own silver-leaf "Lightning Rod" table in the apartment foyer, *near left.*

SCOTT LAMB APARTMENT, BROADWAY

S acramento native Scott Lamb grew up drawing and painting and dreaming of wonderful rooms. "When I was a design student, my scrapbook was filled with photographs of English rooms and English-style houses. The English, particularly in their country houses, have such a feeling for comfort. Unlike most American designers, they appreciate a slight shabbiness and signs of age. For them, the brand-new rooms that haunt our design magazines are reason for grave doubt and suspicion," said Lamb. "I'm looking for a quality of design that lasts. I don't like faddish furniture or trendy design. This translates for me to French, English, and American antiques, Chinese porcelains, fine upholstery, silks, linens, and cottons in soft colors. Then I always add something eccentric and over-scale." ¶ For his Broadway apartment, Lamb first painted the walls a warm canteloupe color. In his ongoing design, an over-scale sofa, topped with down-filled pillows, plus a pair of chintz-covered chairs anchor the room. Ever-changing tabletop collections include museum-quality sculpture and inexpensive personal favorites, like handpainted porcelain vegetables and alabaster fruit.

"I plan rooms that will get even better as they settle in. They should look softer and friendlier with time. Pillows, preferably down-filled, should not be too stiff. Rooms are for living and reading and for entertaining friends. They should not look like stage sets. I'd never design a room using antiques exclusively. It would look like a museum,"said interior designer Scott Lamb.

After first improving the interior architecture of the sunny rooms, Lamb put together his apartment scheme with pretty, muted tones like peach, moss green, pale coral, and cream. Into this setting, he brought the snap of Japanese tables, Chinese porcelains, the delicate tracery of gilt sconces, handpainted screens, and somewhat over-the-top quilted silk curtains on the windows to muffle sound.

Before he flew off to New York to become Director of Creative Services for Polo/Ralph Lauren, designer Jeffrey Walker lived in this sunny, white apartment on the edge of Buena Vista Park. Walker's creamy monochromatic scheme—with its stylized, sculptural furniture, natural canvas upholstery (by Sam Yazzolino), and well-edited objects—confidently pays homage to his mentor, San Francisco designer John Dickinson. ¶ The curvy white-lacquered table (after Jean-Michel Frank), a "Stonehenge" fiberglass lamp, and framed furniture drawings are all by John Dickinson. ¶ Ironstone bowls and platters, gleaming stripped floors, and simple white-on-white upholstery were all Dickinson inspirations. Still, Walker here gives Dickinson's pristine scheme a bold new spin with a spindly Flos lamp next to the mantel, geometric mirrors, and a *faux*-finished stage-set chair of rather grand proportions to take away the room's edginess. An elaborate white-lacquered capital, used here as a table, is a typical Walker tongue-in-cheek touch. It's a fiberglass cast intended for store display. Fat cushions invite guests to sit in the window and take in the view toward the Bay.

John Dickinson once said that all white tones—creamy white, gray-white, and white-white—live happily together. Jeffrey Walker's interior proves that all white is all right. Framed table design drawings and lamp, *above,* by John Dickinson.

Designer Jeffrey Walker muted the mood in his bedroom with a subtle dappled *faux*-marble wall finish, low-slung Roman shades in natural cotton duck, and pale cotton bedcoverings. The custom-designed, over-scale platform bed and matching side-tables are painted matte white. Walker included his techie work desk, task lamps, and upholstered armchair as part of the room, not clumsy intruders. Witty touches here include a French theatrical column that's actually a store display fake, and a white ironstone bowl of natural sponges. Framed architectural drawings were booty from a Venetian holiday. A master of visual effects, Jeffrey Walker used color and scale deftly in his bedroom/studio to create a restful refuge.

The Collectors

"I like to live surrounded by my collections," said designer Robert Hutchinson. "My decorating goal in this apartment is to present favorite things I've gathered over the years in a way that is free and open." Hutchinson first came to San Francisco from Louisiana more than 25 years ago to study with famed art and design teacher, Rudolph Schaeffer. (Michael Taylor and Charles Pfister also studied with Schaeffer, mentor until he died at age 102 for many of the City's finest artists and designers.) ⸿ Highlights of Hutchinson's 30 years of collecting include Mexican and Egyptian masks, Asian burial jars, stone bowls and implements, and African ceremonial masks and stools. ⸿ A museum-quality sculpted greenstone Maori weapon is set on a low shelf in Hutchinson's bedroom. A dramatic king's mask of carved wood from Cameroon stands guard beside his white-linen-covered bed. "Every piece I own has meaning to me. I move them about, walk around them, look at them from all directions, and display them all with great care and appreciation," said the designer. ⸿ Byron Meyer has the same high regard for his paintings and sculpture. Favorite pieces are shuttled from room to room, edited, and sometimes moved out altogether after years of enjoyment and then much introspection. Since our photographs of Meyer's bold collection (page 93) were taken, his Guston and Hudsons and Arnesons have been joined by a small transcendental painting by Ross Bleckner and a graphic painting by Sean Scully. "It's always hard parting with a painting I've loved for years. But I have only so much wall space. I can lend out paintings for shows, but if this collection is going to grow and stay fresh, something has to go," said Meyer, a major supporter of Northern California artists. ⸿ Not all collections start in an art gallery or antique store. Some come from the natural world. Like Ron Mann, Hutchinson finds dramatic rocks on his travels and brings them home. "I get a great deal of pleasure using natural objects. Recently I set an over-scale bamboo tray on a granite table and filled it with river rocks that looked like Henry Moore sculptures. The stones were beautiful. All I had to do was give them a presentation." ⸿ Ron Mann will return from a hike along the rocky Montara shore with spherical speckled rocks that look as if they came from an art studio, or with pale turquoise beach glass. He sets them on weathered wood tables or in newly cast bronze bowls. "Not everything in a room has to be precious," he said.

In designer/collector Robert Hutchinson's city office, favorites are displayed on "floating" shelves. Among his international cast of characters: a Columbian burial jar, Thai terra-cotta heads, coil vessels, Mayan creatures in stone, an Indian seed vessel with a coiled snake, a carved African mask, an Ivory Coast tribal bed, a Korean carved granite pot, and a 200 B.C. Greek road marker.

In Robert Hutchinson's apartment, *opposite,* Mezcala-style stone masks (100 B.C. - 300 A.D.) from Guerrero, Mexico, mounted on the wall and lit by candles. *Center:* Robert Hutchinson (with Michael Carr) "Nicoya" chair, a new three-legged design in wood with hand-finished openwork. *Above:* the front door with textured plaster panels and a gold leaf finish by Michael Carr.

John Dickinson warned against filling rooms with art bought for investment. "Always buy paintings for the pure pleasure. If you must buy art for investment, keep it in a bank vault where it belongs," he growled. ❡ Designer Eleanor Ford also cautions against collecting simply to impress. "It's better to have one fine piece of art than a lot of itsy-bitsy things," she said. "Collections are lovely, but they must be good and well-edited." ❡ Designer Chuck Winslow's interiors (page 124) always have the added spark of contemporary art. "Living with my art collection is like having my best friends around all the time," said Winslow, who has been collecting the works of Billy Sullivan, Robin Bruch, and Stephen Mueller. "I like the visual surprise of a Manuel Neri plaster figure standing beside a pair of Directoire chairs, or a vibrant Tom Holland construction over a Louis XVI fireplace. It's a more personal statement," said the designer, who might also set a beautiful but inexpensive auction find on a precious antique Chinese table. "Contemporary art is one of the few precious things we can still afford to collect," he said. "I always advise clients to buy the very best they can afford. And it's better to purchase a first-rate lithograph than a third-rate painting. Photography can be the beginning of a fine collection for many young people." ❡ Architecture, remarkable paintings and sculpture, and the carefully chosen furniture were the stars, never the bibelots, of Michael Taylor's beautiful rooms. "When in doubt about a room, take out," the great collector (and editor) said. "If a room is in trouble, it's often because there's too much in it. If you can't see the room for the clutter, edit."

When designer Robert Hutchinson bought his two-story storefront property, he discovered it had been built in 1912 with bricks salvaged from the devastation of the 1906 Earthquake. "I set up my studio downstairs and proceeded to renovate upstairs, recreating the rooms for my own pleasure and redecorating all the surfaces," he said. ¶ He spent hours hand-shaping walls out of mud and color and sticks, creating sensuous curves, sculpted shelves, and generous open spaces for his furniture. "It was two years of dabbing and painting and 'ruining' my house, slapping colors up there like some primitive man in his hut. It was my one and only chance to have fun and accomplish something that no client would ever let me do," Hutchinson recalled. ¶ Wall finishes are layers of clay painted with multiple washes to give a centuries-old look. ¶ "As my collections of European arts and crafts—and then African and Asian and South American artifacts—developed, my rooms changed.

Hutchinson's apartment is a lively gallery of his diverse collections. From *left,* a Bob Brady figure, a Stephen De Staebler clay vessel, and Indian mask. African vessels stand on a lignum vitae table top set on a carved Plexiglass base. Hand-painted colors and sticks on the wall are for texture, line, and humor, said the designer. *Above:* a detail of the bathroom with an Aztec figure.

Hutchinson sees his Sutter Street apartment as a laboratory for his ideas. Here, he can use and observe his designs, refine them, edit them, and enjoy each one. ¶ A smooth chunk of lignum vitae tops a Hutchinson-designed curved Lucite base. A great slab of granite stands on a sculpted wood base. A large-scale drafting table is supported by a hand-formed base that looks like slabs of terra cotta. A steel daybed covered with superb Navaho rugs stands in one corner of his office-study accompanied by a remarkable tabletop grouping of ash-gray burial jars, primordial stones, and delicate Indian clay bowls. On a wall nearby, Hutchinson brought a gallery-caliber display to life by creating the illusion that precious Indian bowls are tipping off shelves or falling from a ledge. In fact, they're well-supported by concealed metal supports built into the shelves. Still, his conceit does make visitors look twice at this shapely clay collection. ¶ Here in his apartment, he opened up rooms, created a stair bannister

Hutchinson's collections take over his kitchen, too. A grouping of Indian stone mortars, Central American figures, and river rocks beneath copper pots. In his orchid house, Chinese storage jars, a Mayan salt grinder. "I collect orchids because the flowers are breathtaking but they come from simple, sculptural plants," he said. Favorite orchids: *Brassavolas*.

from smoothly sculpted tree branches, and painted his bathroom walls with a watery wash the color of verdigris. Almost every fixture—door handles, drawer pulls, faucets, shelves, and tabletops—has been designed or hand-sculpted by Hutchinson himself. ¶ He can relax in a sunny roof terrace, cook for company in his spacious kitchen, tend his orchid collection in a sheltered greenhouse, or sculpt a cushy chair to pull up beside the fire, with its remarkable hand-plastered geometric surround. ¶ In his apartment, the designer can introduce his new hand-carved tables and chairs, new ideas for shelves and lighting, critiquing them for weeks before approving them for clients. ¶ Inevitably, since he has so many, prized objects will be retired to a storage room, and others will be brought out to be displayed and appreciated again on tables and shelves. Guided by Hutchinson's free spirit, these rooms will continue to soar.

"I designed the bedroom with all the comforts I could plan in close quarters," said Hutchinson. Beside the bed, a king's mask from Cameroon and a Dogon figure. *Center:* an English japanned red lacquer chest-on-chest. Black lacquer table, chair, and bed are Hutchinson's designs.

When San Francisco Museum of Modern Art trustee Byron Meyer purchased his elegant townhouse atop Russian Hill, the first phone call he made was to interior designer Michael Taylor. Taylor, who once said that the best decoration results from "weeding out," paid a visit. Thus, in 1974, began a year-long design collaboration to rid the 1931 house of its cut-pile carpet, fussy detail, and heavy velvet draperies, and to provide Meyer with the perfect background for his busy life and a first-rate art collection. ❧ Taylor wanted the rooms to have a timeless, international look. First, he pared down and polished the interior architecture, opening doors to create vistas from room to room and cleaning out extraneous moldings, fuss, and trim. ❧ Hardwood floors were left bare or covered with no-nonsense sisal. Sand-textured paints in muted taupe were laid on walls with a trowel to create an authentic antique look. ❧ The same nubby fabric—raw silk with the look of inexpensive burlap—was used in the living room and Meyer's luxurious bedroom. Taylor's signature fossil-stone was used for occasional tables, and for Meyer's remarkable custom-made dining table.

Opposite: A Gilbert & George work on paper, *Rest,* hangs on one wall of the dining room. The table, with stone pedestals, was designed by **Michael Taylor**. *Art Patron Disguised as Local Artisan* by **Robert Arneson** is a tongue-in-chic tribute to Meyer. A Dale Chihuly glass sculpture glows in the center of the oak table beneath an oxidized bronze, *Cone Boy,* by Tom Otterness, *left.*

"My art collection keeps changing because I like to get the newest works by my favorite artists, plus new works by young artists with staying power," said Meyer. ¶ His collection started with paintings by Bay Area figurative painters and now encompasses paintings and sculpture by all major California artists, including Richard Diebenkorn, Robert Arneson, Sam Francis, Ed Ruscha, Billy Al Bengston, Wayne Thiebaud, and Peter Voulkos. "Over the 30 years I've been collecting, I also keep coming back to Paul Wonner, Elmer Bischoff, and Robert Hudson, who were my teachers at night classes at the San Francisco Art Institute. I had to develop my eye, and I learned so much from them," said Meyer. ¶ Collecting Philip Guston in the seventies turned Meyer around and made him search for challenging paintings. Now his collection covers wide territory—from Robert Arneson's sly sculptures to Eric Fischl's sexually charged canvases. He's looking with interest at Man Ray and Joel-Peter Witkin photographs, and exploring the possibilities of video art. ¶ "I really appreciate the luxury of having my favorite paintings around me," admitted Meyer. "They're all here, and I never have to worry that the guard might say, 'I'm sorry, we're closing.'"

Colors of walls and fabrics were muted to emphasise Meyer's carefully curated collection. At *left*, Robert Hudson's painted steel sculpture stands near a window in the living room. Other major works include a Sam Francis painting, *Facing Oil*, Roy De Forest's witty canvas atop the sofa, and a standing bronze by A.R. Penck on the mantel.

The charming but self-effacing lettuce-green exterior of one of the last Victorian houses on Russian Hill gives no hint that the interior contains dramatic John Dickinson-designed rooms with style that Queen Victoria could never have imagined. Nor are there any remaining hints that the house was formerly owned by actress Ina Claire, whose Hollywood-glamorous interior scheme included acres of ruby red carpet and swags of blue silks. ¶ First built in 1861 for a lawyer and his family, the house has spacious rooms of elegant proportions, rosy terra cotta walls, restored Victorian moldings, and a highly personal collection of contemporary ceramics, paintings, and mixed media works by noted California artists. ¶ "When I first started collecting seriously in the late fifties, San Francisco artists who are now internationally recognized were just on the way up. I've bought paintings over the years only by artists I believe in. I'm not interested in being *au courant* or in constantly turning over my collections," said the owner, who noted that her house was not an easy one in which to hang large paintings. Big canvases tend to stay put and anchor a changing display of smaller pieces.

John Dickinson's white-lacquered "Stonehenge" tables and a canvas-upholstered sofa serve as dramatic counterpoints to elaborate lacquered Chinese chests, boudoir chairs, a Biedermeier game table, and a superb lacquered and gilded Queen Anne secretaire. The designer planned the rooms with places to sit with friends, with a book, or beside windows, so that the owners can enjoy green views of their garden and the Art Institute tower through the trees. Among Keesling's collection: ceramics by Rudy Autio, Robert Shaw, and Robert Arneson, and paintings by Frank Lobdell (above sofa), Richard Diebenkorn, Robert Hudson, and Nathan Oliveira.

A white ceramic plate by Pablo Picasso was a gift from Michael Taylor.

I studied drawing with Wayne Thiebaud as a college student, and the first piece I collected was his hand-colored etching of a slice of cake," said Eileen Michael, a patron of the San Francisco Museum of Modern Art. Today, her favorite may be a Manuel Neri plaster figure, or a Roy De Forest oil, but a setting created by Michael Taylor forms the elegant background. ¶ When she first decided to buy her circa 1886 house, it was (like most houses of the Victorian era) dark and uninspiring, with poky rooms but a fine location. ¶ In quick order, she brought in designer Michael Taylor, a family friend, who first had the back wall knocked down and french doors installed. ¶ "Michael Taylor worked in the most inspiring, enthusiastic way. He always had lots of ideas, and he changed them constantly as the room slowly came together. He was a total perfectionist," said Michael. ¶ For her upstairs bedroom, Taylor spent days getting the creamy white color right. ¶ "He'd have the paint applied, then change it the slightest gradation. He'd go home, then come back the next day and perhaps change it again. I'd marvel at his work. It's beautiful in the most subtle way," she said.

One living room wall was enveloped with mirror to increase its apparent size. Taylor-designed chairs and a large melon-shaped ottoman were upholstered with natural-colored linen velvet trimmed with his signature Bouillon cord fringe.

Eileen Michael's bedroom/sitting room was one of the last designs executed by Michael Taylor. Afternoon light pours into the room through Taylor's trademark plantation shutters. In contrast to the large-scale four-poster draped in quilted white linen, Taylor brought together a pair of Diego Giacometti stools, a Michael Taylor-designed travertine table, and an ornate gilt chair upholstered in chartreuse silk. Pablo Picasso lithograph, 1947, *Tete de Jeune Fille* (a portrait of Francoise Gilot). Architect: Sandy Walker.

"Michael always said that the bedroom was the most important room in the house," said Eileen Michael. "He thought you should sit up in bed and feel wonderful." ¶ For her, Taylor designed a quilted-linen-draped bed that's a room within a room. Beside it, he placed two elegant but functional bedside tables with drawers and shelves for books and a telephone, along with fine reading lights. "Michael said that you should be able to go upstairs to your room, light the fire, read in a very comfortable chair, and put your feet up on a table that you couldn't scratch," she recalled. ¶ She appreciated his dedication all the more because the highly successful designer had probably never designed rooms as small as those in her first house. "He brought a lot of large furniture in, but the house never looked cluttered. Michael Taylor was such a talent and so wonderful to work with. But you always had to let him go with his ideas. He did lose his enthusiasm if you tried to tell him what to do."

Living above the store surrounded by his favorite things is the happy lot of antique dealer/interior designer Glen Smith. In 1980, Smith and his G.W. Smith Galleries were pioneers in the Fillmore Street neighborhood that is now bustling with chic restaurants. Making his move from Palm Beach, Smith purchased a pre-Earthquake storefront building with a Japanese fish market at street level and a photography studio upstairs. Still, the spacious second floor had high ceilings and original mantelpieces of cast iron and marbleized enamel that had made the journey from New York around The Horn, and Smith moved in, making few changes. ¶ Today, the upstairs apartment looks as if Smith inherited it from his own travel-mad, antique-collecting family. ¶ In his front parlor, Smith clearly kept many of his best antique pieces for himself. "I've always been fascinated with neoclassical antiquities. That's what I buy for myself," said Smith. "Even when I go to Bali, the pieces I buy have an affinity with Etruscan ceremonial sculpture." ¶ This is neoclassicism that crosses borders. Four Italian Directoire chairs and a fine pair of Biedermeier gondole chairs were upholstered anew in San Francisco, using black cotton printed with a design taken from Greek pottery. Irish, English, French, Italian and American, Indonesian and Greek—even Eskimo—pieces are

Beneath a nineteenth-century neoclassic Swedish mirror, antique dealer Glen Smith displays a crystal obelisk, a first-century Roman head, and a Regency theatrical helmet of tole on an Italian Adam-style marble-topped console table.

A *faux* tortoise table displays an orrery. Four seventeenth-century marble plaques of Roman emperors hang on the wall. The carved wood girandole is of the Adam period. French bronze lamps have Corinthian column bases.

represented and given new life (and company) in this collection. The black-lacquered floor is covered with a pair of Aubusson carpets, their lovely colors further faded by the bright California sunshine. Still, his precious things are made to be used, and his chairs are comfortable as well as remarkable. "I love the purity and simplicity of classic lines. It's not muddled like rococo," said Smith. ¶ He insists that the look and feel of wonderful rooms is a result of thoughtfully arranged furniture. "I place comfortable chairs in groups for conversation, objects on large tables to please the eye, smaller tables beside chairs to hold drinks or books, and desks with good chairs in my bedroom, where I do all my work," he said. ¶ In odd corners of his treasure-filled apartment, he stood vitrines filled with collections of eighteenth-and nineteenth-century tobacco containers, scrimshaw, Indonesian miniatures. On the walls of his study hang colorful framed gouaches of the erupting Vesuvius, as seen by an international cast of painters. ¶ "This is my life. I've devoted my whole life to finding and collecting. But I only buy things I like. That's my rule. To me, it doesn't matter whether they're antique or contemporary if there's perfection in the design. Still, I notice I hardly ever buy anything modern," chuckled Smith.

A pair of 1780 English plaster figures stands on plinths beside a dramatic pair of Ionic columns that originally stood in an Irish country house. Green silk-upholstered Regency gentleman's reading chair by Thomas Hope is inlaid with ebony.

Unique Style

*F*ashion designers Jeanne Allen and Marc Grant can sit outside on the terrace of their hexagonal house in the Berkeley Hills (opposite) and gaze past gnarled pine trees to the San Francisco Bay. Directly below their house is the Campanile on the campus of the University of California. Across the dazzling Bay, beyond Treasure Island, the distant Golden Gate Bridge is stretched between the Presidio and the Marin headlands like a cobweb. ¶ The couple can watch white fog sweep over the Sausalito hills, blot out the bridge, and swirl past the Sutro Tower to shroud the chock-a-block City. ¶ Over in Marin County, a neat twenties house (page 145) is the perfect vantage point for eyeing bobbing boats, a quiet cove, and San Francisco shining like the Emerald City in the clear blue light. ¶ In Cow Hollow (a now-chic preserve named for dairy farms there in the last century), a fashion company executive and his wife enjoy privacy-with-Bay-views in their sunny updated house. ¶ In Pacific Heights, from the windows of a handsome Italianate Victorian (page 138) that may have been built as early as 1865, the view east takes in the City glowing in the morning sun. ¶ On Russian Hill, designer Thomas Bennett can take tea beside the fire (page 141) and watch gray pines buck and sway as the summer fog makes a mad dash down Hyde Street. From his bay window, he might catch a glimpse of the toy-like cable car speeding along its shiny tracks. ¶ San Franciscans have the best of all worlds. They live in one of the most beautiful city settings in the world, in sun-filled houses and apartments within a ten-or twenty-minute drive from glorious Golden Gate Park, museums, the Marina, Sausalito, the walking trails of Marin or the East Bay parks. On weekends they can escape to the quietness and comfort of a hilltop flat to observe the life on the Bay from a distance, or take to the water on a sailboard, yacht, or ferry boat. ¶ San Francisco is a city of friendly neighborhoods, each with its own character and indigenous specialty goods. Residents may shop for freshly roasted coffee, crusty breads, or antipasti in North Beach, then walk a few blocks to Chinatown for bok choy, fresh noodles, branches of colorful spring blossoms, or watercress. ¶ From his apartment above Fillmore Street, David Peugh (page 122) can stroll up the hill as far as Jackson Street to find antiques, Italian footwear, chocolate

Opposite: Despite windows and glass doors on all sides of Jeanne Allen and Marc Grant's house to take in the panorama, the wide overhang allows direct sunlight only at sunrise and sunset. The polished oak floor and a redwood plywood ceiling seem to soak up light and keep the mood inside the rooms somewhat muted. *Overleaf:* With oaks and redwoods to provide privacy, Allen and Grant have left the windows bare. Evenings, the lights of the City glow in the distance.

truffles, Sicilian sausages, used books, hip sunglasses, sushi, vintage clothing, doughnuts, pizza-by-the-slice, and freshly brewed coffee—morning jet fuel for the locals. For respite, he can take in a movie at the Clay theater or meet a friend for lunch at a sunny cafe. ❡ Food is San Francisco's obsession. Stores on every block purvey salad greens, organically grown fruit, ice cream, French pastries, sourdough bread, nine-grain sandwiches, fresh juices. California's bounty is there for everyone to taste. ❡ Friday nights, Elsa Cameron stocks up in the City before driving north into Marin County. Once up there on her sunny perch (page 115), she likes to settle in and cook for friends. Her house in the hills of Marin is so hard to find that she will rendezvous with guests in Fairfax before leading a convoy up the narrow switchback roads to her aerie. On Sunday, she heads back to the City as the setting sun turns the Bay to molten gold. ❡ All this beauty, and houses of character for respite. Who would ever want to leave?

ALLEN AND GRANT HOUSE, BERKELEY HILLS

Nestled in the Berkeley Hills with fine views over San Francisco Bay stands a remarkable 1,200 square-foot hexagonal house designed by Frank Lloyd Wright. The house, owned by San Francisco fashion designers Jeanne Allen and Marc Grant, was originally designed in 1938 as a Malibu beach house but was never built. ¶ Forty years later, a Wright devotee bought the plans from the Frank Lloyd Wright Foundation and proceeded to build the house under the proviso that every detail of the interior and exterior would be faithfully reproduced. At that time, it was the only Wright plan constructed posthumously. ¶ Allen and Grant, feeling the pinch in a decorative but tiny Russian Hill apartment, first heard about the house from one of the carpenters working on it, but never dreamed that they would one day own it. ¶ They observed the construction from a distance as the solid, earthquake-proof foundations were secured on pilings and beams atop 400,000 pounds of gravel. Forty thousand bricks were custom-made—and rejected because the color and size were wrong. Rugs Wright had specified were woven in China. ¶ Soon after the house was completed, they heard from their carpenter friend that it was for sale, with two asking prices—one with furnishings, one without. ¶ Allen and Grant

One early change the couple made was to turn the tiny "bedroom" cubicles (Wright considered sleeping a passive exercise not requiring precious space) into efficient offices where the two often work on weekends. Daytime sofas in the living room unfold into futon beds that can be set up before the fireplace, in a sheltered corner, even on the decks, *opposite,* for summer snoozing. *Left:* Jeanne Allen is a superb chef and loves to cook cracked crab and salads for friends. Since she and Grant spend months each year in Japan designing their fabrics, sushi is another favorite.

On summer days, Allen and Grant throw open doors and windows and barbeque on the deck, *opposite*. In winter, or in foggy August when afternoons are California cool, they bring out sketch books and pens and design their fabrics and fashions before the flickering fire.

Not surprisingly, over the years Allen and Grant have grown to appreciate Frank Lloyd Wright. While they don't regret shipping off those hexagonal stools and museum-quality rugs, they now find themselves on the Wright house-tour circuit—and more intrigued than ever by the Wright mystique.

originally intended to forgo the furnishings, but after lengthy negotiations with the house-proud sellers, they bought the lot. ¶ Since the couple couldn't see living in this enchanted pavilion with Wright's curiously dated color scheme—orange, Easter-basket purple, acid yellow, and lime green—they packed the furnishings and donated them to London's Victoria and Albert museum. ¶ While Allen and Grant admit that "the house looks its best empty," they set about furnishing it with the things they love—Japanese antiques, flea-market finds, family heirlooms, Oriental carpets. Their own easy-to-live-with collage of colors was inspired by tones in Japanese woodblock prints—glossy blacks, rust, gold, gray, warm brown, and navy blue—which complement the raw natural woods particularly well. Many of the tweeds and printed cottons they've used for upholstery are quilted—a signature of their Jeanne Marc fashion collections. ¶ Since Jeanne Allen and Marc Grant travel on business for five or six months a year—much of it in Japan—they find their peaceful house on its quiet hillside street particularly welcoming. The serene setting, along with Wright's obvious admiration for things Japanese throughout the design, smooth the transition from an Osaka apartment to California.

Weekdays, art curator Elsa Cameron lives in a bright yellow Victorian cottage in the Castro, purchased for a song in the sixties. Weekends, she packs her bags and makes a 35-minute dash north to her Fairfax retreat. ❡ With its open-door welcome, sunny colors, crowd-around dining tables, sink-in chairs, and dance-floor-sized deck, the house is like a year-round summer holiday. Furniture with the look of family hand-me-downs are mostly flea-market (even sidewalk) finds, repaired and repainted. ❡ Still, when Cameron first found it, the 1912 summer house suffered from decades of ill-advised renovation and debris from a disastrous storm. For Cameron, who saw the potential and the spectacular views toward Mount Tamalpais, it was love at first sight. ❡ With designer Michael Cyckevic, she recreated her summer cottage with inspiration from Monet's Giverny and the colors of Tuscan afternoons. Open windows and lacy curtains frame her world-class view of the green slopes of Mount Tamalpais.

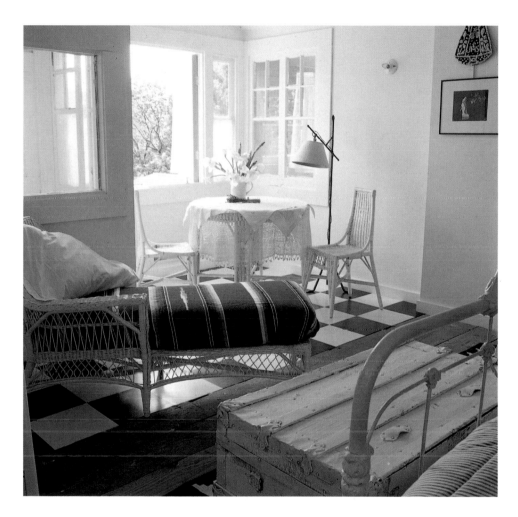

Upstairs in her light-filled, all-white bedroom, Elsa Cameron brought together a restored wrought-iron bed, and old steamer trunk, wicker chairs, and other unusual pieces to create a room that looks as if it has been there since the house was first built.

Treasures brought home from
Mexico add color and zest to
Elsa Cameron's sunny rooms.
The eclectic finds that fill every
shelf and tabletop are like her
extended family.

Signs of wear only add to
the value of Cameron's wicker
and willow chairs. "I like things
that look as if they had a
life before I discovered them,"
said Cameron.

When designer Robert Steffy first saw his Russian Hill house 20 years ago, it had none of the style it has today. "It was so dark inside, you could hardly see. But I did understand its quality and its possibilities. I decided to buy it and work on it," said Steffy, whose wide-ranging talents include designing Italian glass lamp bases, bamboo and *huang hua-li* (rosewood) tables, glass-topped bronze tables, and a new line of tin plates patterned after Chinese export china. "I had my architect draw up plans to remodel the whole house to give us a working scheme, even though I knew it might take years." ¶ He painted all the dark redwood walls and ceilings white and added wrought-iron balconies to the front exterior. A tiny garden was turned into an enchanting dining room, complete with french doors, a striped canvas-shade-covered skylight, and mirrors that reflect bamboo and the pretty peach-colored walls.

The living room looks west to the hills of the Presidio. "I'm very lucky because it's wonderfully lit all day," said designer Robert Steffy. "The sun shines in the garden in the early morning. All afternoon it's bright—I see the sunset. Then in the evening, I can see all the city lights."

As the work progressed, Steffy happened to see a new marble floor in one of the galleries at the California Palace of the Legion of Honor. He searched out the same contractor and designed the bordered pattern for his own dining room. ¶ Steffy's unpretentious and inviting design includes simple natural-canvas-slipcovered chairs and sofas, red-cotton-upholstered Louis XVI chairs, and blue-and-white V'soske rugs on the new oak parquet floors. "If you think I like red, white, and blue, you're right," chuckled Steffy. ¶ Steffy, who attended Parsons School of Design in New York, prefers a crisp look with outlines that won't date.

Over the years, Steffy has added his own designs—Venetian green-glass lamps, a series of tables—but the rooms are still carefully edited and never get cluttered. "I never get bored here," he said. "It's a wonderful house to come home to."

DAVID PEUGH APARTMENT, WESTERN ADDITION

"I think of my apartment style as wacked-out classical. There's a bit of ancient Greece, a little Pompeii, but the materials and finishes are absolutely contemporary," said technical advisor David Peugh of his apartment in the Western Addition. Still, it started life as a tiny one-bedroom shell with no architectural distinction. ¶ Designer Gary Hutton brought in his special offbeat point of view, along with a canny eye for function, and installed hand-cut moldings, a travertine fireplace, and theatrical swags of metallic-painted cotton over sheer voile. ¶ Hutton's tongue-firmly-in-cheek approach spoofs classicism as it spatters new-rage Zolatone over the living room walls, the boxy tables, and even the new kitchen appliances. ¶ To show off Peugh's growing collection of paintings by contemporary California artists, including four large canvases by Joan Brown, Hutton chose a paled-out, tone-on-tone color scheme for each room. Still, there's nothing wishy-washy or still-life about these interiors. As new paintings are added to the prized foursome, the mix only gets better.

David Peugh's apartment is in a new complex, with garden apartments on two levels, plus Trio cafe, gift stores, a dry cleaner, and other neighborhood favorites below fronting Fillmore Street.

Gary Hutton's lighthearted improvisational approach created the look of large-scale rooms with this-minute freshness. The apartment is the perfect stage set for art and antiques.

Night and Day. One apartment, two moods. By day, designer Chuck Winslow's South of Market pied-à-terre is all business. Appointment books, swatches, blueprints, and plans cover his tables and desk. Clients are welcomed, telephone calls are made. Everything he needs to keep his work running smoothly is at hand. ❡ By night, as lights sparkle on the distant Bay Bridge, the efficient office becomes a romantic dining room. Drawings are rolled up and filed away, office equipment is stored. ❡ Lavish flowers and plants from the nearby flower market are set in cache pots and crystal vases, pillows plumped, and the round desk, now a suede-covered dining table, is set with colorful Italian glassware and tall candles. ❡ Lights are dimmed, candles lit, and the music turned on. Italian Consulate-style chairs are exchanged for *faux* tortoise Federal-period chairs. The door bell rings, guests arrive, and champagne corks pop. ❡ With a deft hand, a sure eye, and a generous spirit, Chuck Winslow has transformed this well-located but architecturally undistinguished apartment into a hospitable

Left: Winslow's special mix: Swedish pine chairs, bamboo stools, works by emerging artists, blooms in crystal vases. *Above:* Tall candles and fresh flowers create evening glamor.

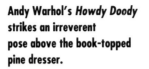
Andy Warhol's *Howdy Doody* strikes an irreverent pose above the book-topped pine dresser.

Seasonal flowers, Venetian glass plates, beeswax candles, French room fragrance, and low light set the stage for conversation and Winslow's down-home cooking.

place for lively conversation and an escape from the everyday world. ¶ First combing and sponging the walls in chameleon taupe and toffee colors that change with the light, he then brought in his favorite objects and paintings, combining periods, perspectives, and materials with verve. An elaborate Chinese antique table, Swedish pine chairs, a pine dresser, witty contemporary art, a growing dog sculpture collection (his favorites are Jack Russell terriers), and Winslow's books are pieces of his life, evidence of hands-on history and Winslow's humor. ¶ No wonder friends feel at home here.

MENDELSOHN HOUSE, RICHMOND DISTRICT

We choose furniture and art that capture our imagination. If we love a piece, we hardly bother with dates, the name of the maker, or its provenance until after we've decided to buy it. Pedigree is simply not our priority," said Barbara and Richard Mendelsohn, who brought together this clever and appealing collection in their grand 1908 shingled house. ¶ Juxtaposed in their rooms are contemporary American and European paintings, an English sideboard (ca. 1840) and a gold-inlaid French cabinet brought from the family house in Johannesburg. To this eclectic mix, they've added a fifties glass-topped table and two remarkable cowhide-upholstered chairs commissioned from California furniture designer Philip Agee, *opposite*. ¶ "We want the furniture to get an emotional reaction. Not everyone likes these pieces, but that's OK. I just don't want our house to look bland or over-designed," said Richard. ¶ In their growing art collection, too, the Mendelsohns like their funny bone tickled. "When we started collecting, we loved realism. Then we moved on to expressionism. Now we're looking for art that's on the cutting edge, more 'out there.' But it must produce an emotional charge, make you laugh, maybe even startle," he said.

The house's art-obsessed owners find their furniture, paintings, and accessories all over the world. Their grand Victorian provides endless wall space, year-round San Francisco light through bay windows, and sumptuous rooms that welcome their changing furniture and canvases.

The four-story Queen Anne-style exterior gives no clue of what's inside. While the proportions and trims of their rooms feel Victorian, the Mendelsohns say that they are really in love with art deco furnishings. Their latest finds are art deco chairs and a table discovered in Paris. "I think this unexpected mix is what San Francisco is really about," said Richard Mendelsohn. "While the exteriors of most houses seem traditional, the interiors are likely to have an edge and be highly individual."

Collections and art find their way into the Mendelsohns' paled-down bedroom, *opposite.* The couple appreciates the bathroom as it is and has no plans to update the fixtures, *right.*

A SHAKER-STYLE HOUSE, COW HOLLOW

The rarity of Shaker collections in San Francisco makes this house a special treat for visitors. The simple lines of the handcrafted treasures are played off against the clean lines of contemporary sofas and chairs upholstered in natural linen/cotton.

Our house is set up on a hill, so we look north over rooftops to the Bay and south to our terraced garden. And we have sunlight throughout the day. Coming from New York, we appreciate openness and light as very special qualities," said the owner, who brought all of her favorite pieces west from a Park Avenue apartment and her Long Island house. ¶ When she and her husband moved to California in 1984 and bought their handsome 1904 shingled house, she first bleached the hardwood floors and painted everything white. After unpacking her fine collection of Shaker antiques, she immediately felt at home. "I've been collecting Shaker and American country pieces for more than 20 years," she said. "These pieces are like my friends. "There's a primitive, almost child-like quality about Shaker and rustic pieces that I love. I respond to the simple, straightforward lines. And I love scrubbed tabletops, things that show signs of wear." ¶ "Total authenticity was never my goal in this house," said the owner, who appreciates Shaker for its purity of line rather than its pedigree. ¶ "I respect my antiques, but I've brought Shaker into the twentieth century. This is a contemporary take, my edited version," she said. The rooms are warm, not at all stiff or intimidating. ¶ Best of all, she provided a seamless, timeless interior setting for her treasures. Sunlight streaming in through mullioned windows and french doors creates its own grid patterns and highlights the friendly charm of her overall design. ¶ Understanding well the strength in repetition, she used the same round white plaster lamps, a nubby sand-colored Canovas linen/cotton, and simple framing for samplers in each setting. "I wanted continuity from room to room. It's very soothing," she said.

Pure white walls and all-day sunshine offer a friendly California welcome to a pencil-post bed, a collection of farm stools, a chest, and framed samplers. Bare floors are very much in the Shaker spirit.

Designer Diane Burn has made a highly successful international career letting her imagination roam free to create interiors of extraordinary charm and wit. In her daughter Adriana's nursery, she made a child's dream of a room, with fairytale characters on walls and heirloom laces on cradle and bed. Her fantasy was created in the high-ceilinged upstairs chamber of an imposing house she renovated, now one of the finest Victorians in the City. Diane, however, is not enamored of the period and has here filled the room with references to other eras. Which eras is a question for the enchanted visitor—and Diane's blonde daughter—to answer.

In New York, Porto Ercole, and Los Angeles, designer Diane Burn has created fantasy interiors with *boiserie,* exquisite plastering, tea-dipped silks and muslins, period furnishings, and an eye finely tuned to nuances of color. Here, for her daughter Adriana, she commissioned artist Ami Magill to paint storybook murals in the dreamy nursery.

The late afternoon sun streaks through old window shutters into designer Tom Bennett's Russian Hill sitting room. Only the occasional cheery click and clang and clatter of the cable car speeding along Hyde Street line give a clue that the room is in San Francisco. Baize-green walls, Asprey shagreen boxes, a fine Baktiari rug, garden roses, a Louis Seize chair before a Directoire architect's table, Bennett's collection of dog prints, and sculptural mounted trophies suggest an Englishman's hunting lodge—in France. ¶ To create this cozy setting, the young designer gathered together a lifetime's collection and wrote his own life story. "I like a room that tells you something about the person who lives here," said Bennett, who insists he's no longer as enthusiastic about blood sports as his collection might suggest. "As my enthusiasms change, the room will evolve within this scheme I've set up. Chairs will come, I'll see something better, and the old will go. Fabrics may change. Design is a process, not an end in itself. Rooms should never be static." Bennett happily mixes flea-market finds with family treasures to create his charming "young fogey" room.

Designer Tom Bennett mixed periods, countries, and provenance to give his Russian Hill apartment its point of view. Baize-green walls are the moody background for his relaxed style. Garden roses in an etched crystal case, a scrimshaw, and shagreen box collection are displayed on a walnut Directoire chest of drawers. Silk velvet upholstery, cashmere throws, and comfortable chairs complete the composition.

Drifts of linens, pillows, and coverlets hand-embroidered with Binche, Venise, Cluny, and Battenberg laces cover the beds—and almost everything else—in Jan Dutton's sunny Fairfax house. Clearly, white linen is the most romantic—and versatile—fabric. ¶ Inspired by her love of fine white linens, Dutton founded Paper White nine years ago to manufacture and sell her diaphanous designs. Her company has been a raging success, and these fabrics of fantasy are available (and copied) all over the world. No one, it seems, is immune to the charms of delicate lace-edged and hand-embroidered linens. ¶ In her hillside house, Dutton is most generous with her beautiful white linen. She upholsters chairs and sofas with it, swathes her four-poster with it, dresses tables with the lovely stuff, and uses it quite conventionally as curtains, pillow covers, pristine aprons, and timeless dresses.

Paper White designs have the look of heirlooms, but they're newly produced in the finest Belgian and Italian linens. Jan Dutton insists that even white-linen-upholstered chairs are practical as well as decorative. She should know. She has two young boys. Fresh flowers, the scroll of a hand-carved chair leg, lunch on the terrace, and the leafy paradise outside her windows are visions of another era against this dreamy white background.

When we first saw our house in 1974, it was pretty forlorn. It had been damaged by a storm, then stood vacant for five years until we came upon it and knew its potential," said the owner of this charming house, which was built in 1920 in the best tradition of the Northern California craftsman style. With its remarkable views of the Bay and the distant spires of the City, it's also within walking distance of the town of Tiburon and the ferry. ¶ After first repainting and replastering their hillside house, the owners—a lawyer and his wife, the editor of the local newspaper—called in a friend, architect Howard Backen. His firm's clients include the likes of filmmakers George Lucas and Robert Redford. Backen drew up a masterful plan for their 1,750 square-foot house, and supervised a remodel that eventually enlarged it to a spacious 2,850 square feet. ¶ "We wanted the floor plan of the house improved but didn't want to lose the twenties feeling," said the owners.

Interior walls were removed and windows enlarged to give a real sense of place. Clear light fills the house all day; in the afternoon, the sun seems to reach into every corner. The newly renovated rooms are superbly proportioned and thoughtfully organized. Now you can see the view—surely one of the most beautiful in the world—from all the rooms upstairs.

This Marin County house sits on a small lot, so the owners added decks off the living room and the master bedroom downstairs. Painted floor in the kitchen, *opposite,* is by Patricia Dreher. Rooms in this Tiburon house were furnished simply, comfortably, and with great charm. Pale colors form an empty canvas for patterns of changing light. Shuttered interior windows above a work counter in the remodeled kitchen invite the view, too.

Architect Howard Backen's redesign for this Tiburon house included moving the entrance from the front to the side, adding an internal staircase that gives direct access to the center of the house, and adding new floors of vertical-grain Douglas fir. ¶ The new dining area, formerly the sun porch, sits right out in front of the house with a view of Belvedere Cove, Belvedere, and the City. ¶ A square motif is reiterated on wainscotting, atop picture windows, as door trim, and along the bannisters. Pale background colors that seem to glow in the sunlight further emphasize the friendly scale of the rooms and their extraordinary natural setting.

The master bedroom, *opposite,* was created from an unfinished basement. Now it opens to a gracious lattice-shaded deck. Howard Backen updated the interiors with reverence for the original craftsman style. The owners' heirlooms fit right in.

Chuck Williams sometimes jokes that his 1906 cottage is "too tiny to spend much time in," but the likes of Julia Child and James Beard have often joined him there around the dining table. ❡ The shingled cottage, hidden away in a leafy cul-de-sac, was originally built in Golden Gate Park as shelter for 1906 Earthquake victims. San Francisco city fathers later decided that those living in the "earthquake cabins" could have them if they moved them onto their own land. This one arrived on the slopes of Nob Hill via horse-drawn dray. ❡ Williams, the founder of kitchenware purveyors Williams-Sonoma, bought the four-roomed house in the sixties. First order of business was to excavate beneath the structure to create what is now, literally, the ground floor. It's here that Williams spends much of his time, cooking in his unpretentious open kitchen and entertaining friends.

Designed so that his friends can gather around as he chops, Chuck Williams' kitchen is well-equipped with a lifetime's collection of practical cookware—but nothing flashy. His 30-year-old gas stove has more than earned its keep and is there to stay. On his eighteenth-century dresser, he has arranged vignettes of fresh fruits and vegetables, Lunéville ceramics, and Chinese porcelains.

FREDERICK HILL APARTMENT, LAFAYETTE PARK

In literary agent Frederick Hill's apartment overlooking San Francisco Bay, books are the heart and soul of the rooms. In the living room, one whole wall is covered with books neatly lined up on redwood shelves. A reflection in the gilt-framed *belle époque* cafe mirror doubles the apparent length of the floor-to-ceiling collection. An antique library table and sturdy old wooden library ladder complete the bibliophile's room. "My goal is to have all my walls covered with books by the best contemporary American writers, including many by my clients," said Hill. "The minimalist look is not for me. I like to have my favorite things around to enjoy every day." ¶ Starting with a few antique pieces, his lifetime collection of books, and the expertise of designer Chuck Winslow, Hill has given his one-bedroom apartment in a twenties building his individual stamp. One masterstroke was the choice of the rich marmalade color for the striéd walls. Painter Carole Lansdown also gave the fireplace its distinctive *faux marbre* finish. Pearl-gray, pigskin-suede-upholstered Louis XVI chairs, Knoll end tables, and an unholstered tweed screen outlined in nailheads are part of his eclectic mix. Hemp diving-board floor matting was chosen for looks and durability. Hill shares his apartment with a rambunctious Hungarian puli.

Frederick Hill's apartment, on a hill near Lafayette Park, offers grandstand views of the Bay and two bridges. The mottled marmalade-colored walls keep the north-facing apartment sunny and bright during the day and glamorous at night. With the "bones" in place, Hill will continue to see his rooms as works in progress. Still, favorite objects like the gilt-framed study by nineteenth-century American painter William Norton, Masai photographs by Carole Beckwith, and inviting down-filled sofas will always stay.

Across the Bay from San Francisco stands a bucolic Berkeley property discovered by a local artist in 1976. Formerly part of a large estate, the cow barn/granary/milking shed/hayloft was originally designed in 1908 by John Galen Howard, the campus architect for the University of California Berkeley from 1905 to 1930. ¶ With thoughtful renovation by architect Chuck Trevisan, the old barn is now the home of the artist's family. Down the hill, a horse barn eventually became their guest cottage. "I don't think Howard would recognize these buildings even though they're remodelled in the style, spirit, and symmetry of the original," said Trevisan. ¶ A shady colonnade was added and later enclosed to create a family room and bedroom. A new swimming pool and patio were built by the artist, his wife, and their three sons, using old bricks and tiles from the property. A new pergola and trelisses covered with wisteria ensure privacy. ¶ Still in the planning stages are a new dining room and a renovation of the kitchen. In the meantime, the family's glorious acre offers them the very best retreat just 20 minutes from the City.

"We repaired and updated all the old buildings on the property without changing their style or scale. They had to look as if they had always been there," said architect Chuck Trevisan, who planned the changes. Sheltered by stands of eucalyptus and a redwood grove, the property includes a new swimming pool and patio and a retro-new house, formerly a barn.

For 60 years, this is where the estate's former gardener milked the cows, tended his trees, and kept the wells working. In the spirit of Howard's rustic structure, Trevisan has guided its metamorphosis into a 2,000-square-foot cottage with light, comfort, and all modern conveniences.

Behind a "tough" exterior—black asbestos tile walls, perforated-metal garage doors—stands one of the most elegant contemporary interiors in San Francisco. While the simplicity and machine-made ethic may appear Early Bauhaus, the accent is on fine craftsmanship and the luxury of hands-on finishes. ¶ "The key here is the contradictions. Dan Solomon's architectural design is pure and refined, but the materials we chose were complex to install or apply," said the owner, composer Pat Gleeson. His wife, Joan Jeanrenaud, is cellist with the Kronos Quartet. ¶ Sound-softening punched-metal wall panels look to him at times like the "skin" of a 1947 DC-3, and in daylight have the subtle play of light and color of Monet's water lily paintings. A series of metal bolts attaches each panel to plywood panels on the wall surfaces. ¶ Interior designer Terry Hunziker's subtle color scheme juxtaposes warm charcoal leather and grey/beige wool serge upholstery, raw-steel table bases, and rich taupe lacquered wood. ¶ Leather-covered sculptural chairs with rakish angles by Stanley Jay Friedman are a distillation of classical forms. ¶ The inner

Preceding pages show the barrel-shaped stairwell of the Gleeson/Jeanrenaud house, with its pearl-gray hand-plastered walls. Sunlight through the front windows creates ever-changing light patterns. *Opposite:* In the living room, Seattle interior designer Terry Hunziker first planned a modular "ledge"—12-inch wide shelves and jutting tables—in steel with metallic-overlaid laquered oak. Hunziker's sofas and daybed are upholstered in handsome gray/beige serge. Articulated lamp by Artemide. Photograph, *left,* by Robert Mapplethorpe. Framed construction, *right,* by Bruce Conner. Windows give glimpses of the City skyline.

core of the house is lit by a large domed skylight. A circular stairway of painted steel-plate gives access to the master bedroom loft and an all-zinc master bathroom. ❡ Counter-tops and cabinet door fronts in the kitchen are covered with sheets of zinc. On a lower level are two practice studios. ❡ Designer Hunziker drew up furniture that is at once softly sculptural and blocky with complex interlocking shapes and surprising surfaces. "Dan Solomon provided me with wonderful spaces to work with, a blank canvas," he said. Sofas, tables, chairs, and banquettes follow a low horizontal line below sensuous perforated-metal walls. "The solid, weighty, complex patterns happen below an airy, reflective surface. The room's visual power comes from this look of 'sky' above and 'landscape' below," mused Hunziker. ❡ This is custom design at its best, and the couple's delight in living and working within this creation is very evident. ❡ "I love the paradoxes. The robust structural severity, the single-minded 'industrial' approach are very Beethoven, but the refinement, wit, and subtle shifts are move like Ravel," Gleeson said.

Victoriana

Golden afternoon light shines down on San Francisco, spotlighting rows of Victorian houses that cling to the green hills and climb up impossibly steep slopes. Over in Marin County, the clear Northern California light casts its glow on a cheery yellow Victorian house surrounded by flower-covered decks and almost a century of history. ❡ On Russian Hill, a tiny Victorian now in the shadow of tall apartment buildings casts off years of benign neglect and gains fresh all-white interiors. ❡ In the Alexander Valley, a venerable Victorian stands amid rows of vines and looks down the valley with a certain hauteur. ❡ In Pacific Heights, on a quiet tree-lined street, a beautifully tended shingled Victorian belonging to a painter received the John Dickinson treatment. Dickinson's plan for the upstairs bedroom—herringbone-tweed-covered walls, a steel-pipe four-poster—rocked the design world. Queen Victoria may have been amused. ❡ A historic Victorian house in Sonoma County found an energetic new owner and designer, who dressed the old girl in new clothes and took her dancing. ❡ No matter where the visitor wanders in San Francisco, Victorian houses stand in line, catching the eye with their powerful symmetry and rainbow-colorful detailing. ❡ Victorians dating back as far as 1870 grace the perimeter of Alamo Square. A trio of rare Queen Anne tower houses gaze out over the Bay on Pacific Avenue, between Octavia and Laguna streets. Some Victorians are tiny gingerbread cottages, others (like the Haas-Lilienthal House) stand as tribute to the craft and art of wooden-house building. ❡ Built at a fast clip between 1870 and 1906 of abundant coastal redwood, the house exteriors were carved, pressed, sawed, ornamented, "signed," incised, and embellished, then painted, to a fare-thee-well. ❡ Victorians that survived the 1906 Fire range in style from the stately Italianate villa to the gable-roofed Queen Anne, quirky Gothic Revival, strictly tailored San Francisco Stick, and the rustic pretensions of the many Eastlake variations. All packed a lot of detail into typical narrow "shotgun"-shaped San Francisco lots. And almost all turned a very decorative face to the street. Once past the false parapets and five-sided bay windows, however, style stops. Sides and backs of the houses are rather mundane. ❡ Happy in their artifice, Victorians put on a wonderful show. And to view them, all you need is a map or guide book, and a cable car or bus ticket.

Harry and Maggie Wetzel, both active in the arts and music worlds in San Francisco, can relax on the porch of their Victorian house in the Alexander Valley and enjoy the view. Over vineyards of cabernet and chardonnay grapes, they see beyond the Russian River. Their house has had many lives. The present structure was constructed around 1906 with redwood from an 1846-1848 house damaged in the 1906 Earthquake. "Gingerbread" on the porch is the 1906 original.

WETZEL HOUSE, ALEXANDER VALLEY

On a beautiful site surrounded by Alexander Valley Vineyards land, the Wetzels' refurbished house, *opposite,* is ready to face another century. The property was first settled around 1840, when the valley was a challenging two- or three-day journey north from the very young town of San Francisco.

Maggie and Harry Wetzel's Alexander Valley Victorian looks as if it has been snoozing in the Northern California sun for decades, keeping an eye on the changing seasons, watching the vineyards flourish. ¶ The picturesque house's history is rather more lively. Cyrus Alexander first settled the valley around 1840, and in 1848 (with the Gold Rush in full cry), built an adobe and timber home to house his large family. The dramatic 1906 quake split the walls asunder, so in 1906, he dispensed with the adobe and built a new house, using the same redwood timbers. The builders used plans purchased from a lumber supply company, Maggie Wetzel guesses, and added their own "gingerbread" embellishments. ¶ The Wetzels, then living in Los Angeles, purchased the 650-acre property in 1963. This house, until then owned by the Alexander family, was handsome but in need of renovation. Keeping to the original floor plan, the Wetzels opened rooms by removing walls and eliminating dark hallways. Exterior redwood timbers were removed, cleaned, replaced, and repainted. All original fireplaces, in fine functioning order, were kept in place. New wiring and a modern kitchen were added. ¶ The Wetzels did not want to disturb the fine century-old fig trees, so the exterior today looks exactly as it did in 1908.

Rooms, *above and opposite,* are
furnished in Victorian style,
with an eye for comfort and
charm rather than period
authenticity. Interior design by
Sandy Salmon.

Maggie Wetzel, who loves to garden, restored old beds of lilacs, rhododendrons, heirloom roses, ancient olives, fruiting mulberries, and figs. A large vegetable garden supplies the house with year-round fresh salads and herbs.

TOBY LEVY REDESIGN, RUSSIAN HILL

A new take on Victorian, this living room suggests formality with its precise placement of furniture and minimal details. A pair of new black-lacquered sofas was designed by New Yorker Steven Holl. An elaborate mirror was discovered in an antique store in Mexico. The owners' imposing mahogany sofa was an impulse purchase from the house's previous owner, an opera singer. *Opposite:* Not all Victorians are fussy, cluttered, and abuzz with pattern. A fine, white-marble mantelpiece set the monochromatic color scheme for this large Russian Hill living room. Afternoon light from west-facing bay windows illuminates subtle details like the rich Jacquard pattern of upholstery fabrics, quirky floor planks, and sculptural furniture shapes. Scandinavian gilt stools from Therien and Co. Collage by Joseph Raffael. Silver candlesticks by Swid-Powell from Fillamento.

Victorian houses don't have to be dark, stodgy, or uncomfortable," said young architect Toby Levy, whose crisp, focused renovation revitalized this 1896 house for its new owners. The small white house, squeezed between two apartment buildings on the crest of Russian Hill, was formerly a period piece of tiny, cluttered rooms. The living room, which now measures 17 1/2' x 27', was carved out of two small bedrooms. To fill this room with sunshine, Levy restructured and widened its bay window. Stripping away extraneous moldings, carpet, and trim, Levy opted for a monochromatic scheme, strictly edited. ¶ With its marble mantelpiece, white-upholstered sofas by New Yorker Steven Holl, stripped floors, and formal arrangement, the room celebrates the best of Victorian and modern without getting stuck in exact replication. Nor did the architect attempt to make it look like a new house. Watermarks and random planking on the hardwood floors, plus old windows and bannisters, are its endearing signs of old age.

RALPH DU CASSE HOUSE, PACIFIC HEIGHTS

Artist Ralph Du Casse made the most of the terrace garden for his cedar-shingled 1882 Queen Anne house. From his sunny verandah, he looks onto a trimmed English box knot garden shaded by *Pittosporum* trees. Two iron urns stand at the corners. ❡ John Dickinson's dramatic design for Du Casse's bedroom (*overleaf*) was completed in 1968, but looks as startlingly original today. Walls upholstered with herringbone wool tweed bordered with brass strips set the stage for a 12-foot four-poster bed fabricated of industrial steel pipes and outlined with brass. The steel pipes were finished and rubbed to look like pewter. In a more Victorian mood are "antimacassar" shades of crocheted cotton. ❡ Du Casse's bedroom suite was the only part of the house Dickinson designed. Elsewhere, the painter mixes Victorian, Regency, Chinese, and Italian antiques in chic rooms of silky comfort.

Cream-colored paint ices the best features of Du Casse's shingled house. His garden, *opposite,* is a symmetrical oasis of calm.

The tweed bedcover is lined with summer-weight camel-colored cashmere. Bedside tables are covered with a wool Jacquard, which repeats the carpet motif in miniature. Glove-leather chairs with hand-carved "twig" legs were also designed by John Dickinson. Du Casse, an imaginative collector, has added a few pieces over the years, but the bedroom is essentially as John Dickinson designed it more than 20 years ago.

JUDY AND PETER SEVERSON HOUSE, MARIN COUNTY

In a wooded peninsula that juts out into the Bay is one of San Francisco's hidden treasures. It's also home to some of the most costly real estate in the world. With million-dollar views in all directions, mansions and estates enjoy a rare privacy, thanks to narrow, winding roads that discourage visitors. ¶ This is the quiet haven where Judy and Peter Severson, their son, Christopher, (and two Airedales) found their splendid Victorian house, *opposite,* with its close-up views of the water and vistas to Tiburon and Angel Island. ¶ The house was built as a summer cottage in 1892, but it had been cared for lovingly over the years by the six families who called it home. ¶ The Seversons live surrounded by the richness of its history. Stained-glass windows, woodwork, trims, and floors are all original.

Gracious rooms with generous doorways, *this page,* give the house its comfort and character. The family has filled terraces and decks, *opposite,* with pots of citrus, agapanthus, and flowering vines beside a flourishing hillside garden.

With great appreciation of their hillside house and the Victorian tradition, the Seversons furnished it with inherited pieces. Their special feeling for the past is everywhere evident. ❡ Oriental carpets pattern hardwood floors. An ornate Victorian table stands in the entrance hall topped with a celadon bowl of fragrant potpourri. Delicate laces on the windows enhance this nostalgic setting. ❡ It's here in her attic studio that Judy Severson creates printed "quilts" on paper, using embossing to duplicate the whitework of quilting. Her growing business now includes quilt-motif notecards, frameable prints, and a stationery collection. Traditional quilt patterns include "Rose of Sharon," "Morning Glory Wreath," "Spring Tulips," and "Birds in Flight."

Open decks and balconies of Judy and Peter Severson's house allow them to enjoy life on the water year-round. In each sun-filled room, the family has brought together English antiques and handed-down pieces to give rooms a period feel without slavish recreation of the heavy-handed Victorian style.

Blooms Judy brings in from
her garden are often fragrant
heirloom roses, and she fills
vases with cottage-garden
pansies, daisies, and pink phlox.
Her dressing table, *right*,
stands in front of a window
that looks directly over the Bay.
Judy's love of quilts is
very evident in the bedroom.
Quilting hoops hang on a
quilt rack. Quilt on the bed is
her own work.

Originally built in 1850 for the owners of the first winery in Sonoma County, this picture-perfect house was given new life by its owner, San Francisco theatre impresario Steve Silver, and interior designer Gary Hutton. ¶ "My client wanted the interiors to be casual and comfortable, with calm colors. He leads a hectic life in the City and loves to escape to his country house less than an hour from the Golden Gate Bridge," said Hutton, who grew up on his grandfather's apple ranch on the Monterey Peninsula. ¶ Overgrown trees crowded the house when its latest owner first arrived. The scene was a grim one. Landscape architect Edward Nicholas cleared trees and rampant undergrowth to reveal the charming symmetry of this early Victorian house, surely the oldest represented in this volume. ¶ "There was no view visible from the rooms, and the interiors were quite drab," said the designer, who eventually removed tacky moldings and had everything—including a knotty pine kitchen—painted white. Oak floors were bleached. ¶ All sofas and chairs were slipcovered in favorite hot-weather fabrics like blue-and-white-striped French linen, and pale-blue linen/cotton. The effect is crisp and rather tailored. ¶ The owner's growing collection of blue-and-white china is displayed in almost every room.

White wicker chairs discovered in a Sonoma antique store invite relaxation on the verandah. From the widow's walk on the roof, San Francisco is visible—on a clear day.

The bevelled glass in the front doors is original to the house. Silver's "Blue Willow" pattern collection stands on Ralph Lauren wicker tables.

Morning sun fills the office/television room with light. Crackled lacquer table by Therien and Co. Muted colors in the room are accented by a striped linen/cotton-upholstered sofa.

At one end of Silver's living
room, a grouping includes
a hand-carved wood model for
a barrel table, antique-iron
flower baskets, and an Eastlake
Victorian chair.

Designer Gary Hutton set a relaxed mood in the living room with cool cotton/linen slipcovers, fat pillows, and sisal carpet. The coffee table has a lacquered linen finish. White-lacquered tin fireplace was original to the 1850 house. A *faux* stone lamp by Randolph & Hein.

For the dining room, Hutton and Silver devised an all-white scheme. Around the table covered with painters' canvas dropcloths stand white-painted Louis XVI chairs. French doors open to the garden for summer entertaining. Terra cotta figure, Elsa Peretti terra cotta candlesticks, and potted boxwood are arranged on the summertime dining table.

A grand staircase leads to the five bedrooms upstairs. A second stair leads on up to the widow's walk on the roof.

Nine framed etchings of Spanish bullfights are mounted above the bed in the guest bedroom, *opposite*. A forties bed was painted white and striéd with blue by the owner.

In the main bedroom, the same pale color scheme provides a restful background for a handsome wicker bed with white linens, and for an odd pair of chairs previously used on a set for the cult movie *Harold and Maude.* Plaster wine jug lamps designed by John Dickinson.

San Francisco's surprise is that it transcends all clichés. Perched on the Pacific Rim, it seems rather prim and European but offers the very best of open-air California living. With year-round spring weather, the City affords green vistas, billowing fog, piercing white light, and a bevy of *beaux arts* buildings and Victorian houses that look brand new. ¶ Design stores stock superb contemporary furniture, Mexican glassware, English gardening tools, Navaho rugs, California crafts, Italian linens, Chinese porcelains, French fabrics, American antiques, and Japanese sculpture—with San Francisco verve. ¶ The San Francisco Catalogue celebrates the diversity of the City's museums, art galleries, stores, designers, walking tours, and historic houses. ¶ Discover a new museum, tour the galleries, downtown and neighborhoods, then shop to take some San Francisco Style home.

MUSEUMS:

Asian Art Museum
Golden Gate Park,
San Francisco,
(415) 668-8921
A superb, beautifully presented collection of the finest Asian arts.

California Palace of the Legion of Honor
Lincoln Park,
34th Avenue
and Clement Street,
San Francisco,
(415) 750-3659
Paintings, sculpture, and decorative arts by artists from the European schools, superbly displayed in a neoclassical building donated to the City by Alma de Bretteville Spreckels. Cafe Chanticleer.

M.H. de Young Memorial Museum
Golden Gate Park,
San Francisco,
(415) 750-3659
The City's largest art museum, with an emphasis on American art from Colonial times to the twentieth century. Also features arts of Oceania, Africa, and the Americas. Cafe de Young has a pretty garden terrace.

Jewish Community Museum
121 Steuart Street,
San Francisco,
(415) 543-8880
Explores Jewish art and culture, and traditions throughout the ages. Also focuses on developing and presenting young talent.

Judah L. Magnes Museum
2911 Russell Street,
Berkeley,
(415) 849-2710
Permanent collection of art and artifacts of Jewish culture. Travelling exhibitions.

Situated across the Golden Gate Bridge in the beautiful 13,000-acre Golden Gate National Recreation Area, Headlands Center for the Arts is a wonderful discovery for the adventurous art lover. This non-profit interdisciplinary laboratory for the arts, founded in 1982, is headquartered in a formerly deserted 1907 army barracks remade as a series of functional environments by artists, including David Ireland, and architect Mark Mack. Artists live and work here, and special events and shows are held throughout the year. For information and directions, call (415) 331-2787. Photograph by Mark Klett.

Mexican Museum
Building D, Fort Mason,
San Francisco,
(415) 441-0404
Lively shows in all media.
Excellent shop.

Museo Italoamericano
Building C, Fort Mason,
San Francisco,
(415) 673-2200
Celebrates Italian art,
culture, and lives.

Oakland Museum
1000 Oak Street,
Oakland,
(415) 273-3401
California art
collections—including
history and science
departments—in a
dramatic Kevin
Roche designed building.
Public garden and cafe.

San Francisco Art Institute
800 Chestnut Street,
San Francisco,
(415) 771-7020
Changing shows in an art
school's historic building.
Be sure to visit the Diego
Rivera gallery.

San Francisco Craft and Folk Art Museum
Landmark Building A,
Fort Mason,
San Francisco,
(415) 775-0990
A gem. Imaginative
shows in a historic
complex.

Left: White leather and laquered wood chair (circa 1978) designed by John Dickinson. Collection of the San Francisco Museum of Modern Art. (Gift of Mrs. Paul Wattis.)

San Francisco Museum of Modern Art
401 Van Ness Avenue at
McAllister Street,
San Francisco,
(415) 863-8800
The first museum on the
West Coast devoted to
twentieth-century art now
has a permanent
collection of over 13,000
pieces, including
painting, sculpture,
photography, and media
art. New Department of
Architecture and Design
programs and shows
include furniture and
product design, graphic
design, and interior
design. New Mario
Botta-designed museum
building to open on Third
Street, south of Market
Street, in 1993.

University Art Museum
2626 Bancroft Avenue,
Berkeley,
(415) 642-1207
University of California at
Berkeley museum shows
eclectic exhibitions in a
bold concrete building
designed by San
Francisco architect Mario
Ciampi. Cafe.

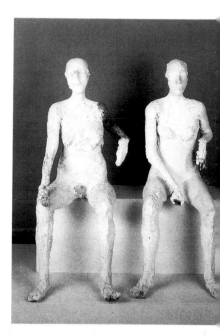

Mary and Julia, pigmont and plaster figures by San Francisco sculptor Manuel Neri. Collection of the San Francisco Museum of Modern Art. A gift of Agnes Cowles Bourne. Photograph by Don Meyer.

A SELECTION OF ART GALLERIES OF SPECIAL NOTE:

The downtown area delineated by Grant Avenue, Sutter Street, Geary Boulevard, and Union Square contains most of the fine art galleries in San Francisco, but art aficionados will also discover galleries South of Market, in North Beach and Pacific Heights, at Fort Mason, and around the Performing Arts Center. Most of these galleries show contemporary paintings and sculpture, and a tour of ten or fifteen or more will offer a fine overview of what's happening in the California art world.

Allrich Gallery
251 Post Street,
San Francisco,
(415) 398-8896
Fiber artists, new works.

Gallery Paule Anglim
14 Geary Boulevard,
San Francisco,
(415) 433-2710
Paintings and sculpture with international scope.

Artspace
1286 Folsom Street,
San Francisco,
(415) 626-9100
International shows; owners encourage avant garde works.

John Berggruen Gallery
228 Grant Avenue,
San Francisco,
(415) 781-4629
In his two-level gallery, Berggruen shows gilt-edged works of acclaimed California artists, along with twentieth-century masters. John Berggruen also shows sculpture at his gallery in the Monadnock Building, 685 Market Street, San Francisco, (415) 495-6850.

Rena Bransten Gallery
77 Geary Boulevard,
San Francisco,
(415) 982-3292
Paintings, sculpture, international artists.

Braunstein/Quay Gallery
250 Sutter Street,
San Francisco,
(415) 392-5532
California contemporary works, international scope.

Capp Street Project
65 Capp Street,
San Francisco,
(415) 626-7747
Artists are given two-month residencies in this David Ireland-designed house. You may visit the resulting works.

Joseph Chowning Gallery
1717 17th Street,
San Francisco,
(415) 626-7496
Paintings, sculpture, ceramics, drawings by leading California artists.

Contemporary Realist Gallery
506 Hayes Street,
San Francisco,
(415) 863-6550
Gallery owners Michael Hackett and Tracy Freedman curate imaginative shows, often with provocative works by local architects.

Crown Point Gallery
871 Folsom Street,
San Francisco,
(415) 974-6273
Artists are invited to make prints with Crown Point, and some of their work is on show.

Michael Dunev Gallery
77 Geary Boulevard,
San Francisco,
(415) 398-7300
Contemporary American, European, and South American art.

Victor Fischer Gallery
30 Grant Avenue,
San Francisco,
(415) 433-4414
Sculpture, paintings.

Fraenkel Gallery
55 Grant Avenue,
San Francisco,
(415) 981-2661
Fine photography.

Fuller-Gross Gallery
228 Grant Avenue,
San Francisco,
(415) 982-6177
Paintings and sculpture by leading contemporary California artists.

Gump's Gallery
250 Post Street,
San Francisco,
(415) 982-1616
Changing shows in the venerable store.

Ianetti-Lanzone Gallery
310 Grant Avenue,
San Francisco,
(415) 956-6646
Paintings and sculpture in a bold new gallery.

Ivory/Kimpton Gallery
55 Grant Avenue,
San Francisco,
(415) 956-6661
Contemporary paintings.

Erika Meyerovich
231 Grant Avenue,
San Francisco,
(415) 421-9997
Provocative international
shows.

Modernism
685 Market Street,
San Francisco,
(415) 541-0461
Paintings and sculpture;
highly individual.

**William Sawyer
Gallery**
3045 Clay Street,
San Francisco,
(415) 921-1600
California artists.

Jeremy Stone
23 Grant Avenue,
San Francisco,
(415) 398-6535
Paintings and sculpture in
a new gallery.

Dorothy Weiss
256 Sutter Street,
San Francisco,
(415) 397-3611
Ceramic sculpture,
drawings, paintings.

James Willis Gallery
109 Geary Boulevard,
San Francisco,
(415) 989-4485
Tribal art from Asia,
Oceania, Africa.

Stephen Wirtz
345 Sutter Street,
San Francisco,
(415) 433-6879
Paintings, sculpture,
photography.

In addition to its original David Ireland-designed house, *above,* **the Capp Street Project/AVT now includes a 10,000 sq. foot former auto-detailing shop for permanent exhibitions, lectures, performances, screenings and other events. Photograph by M. Lee Fatherree.**

FIVE VICTORIANS TO VISIT:

Visitors can do more than stroll past Victorians and gaze longingly at the windows, hoping to be invited in. Five have been preserved as museums and may be visited. Be sure to telephone for hours and special events.

Camron-Stanford House
1418 Lakeside Drive,
Oakland,
(415) 836-1976
A graceful Italianate
mansion, originally built
in 1875. Exhibits describe
Victorian techniques of
wood graining, cut glass,
plaster work, stencilling,
and milling.

Dunsmuir House and Gardens
2960 Peralta Oaks Court,
Oakland,
(415) 562-0328
A 37-room Colonial
Revival mansion set in
40-acre grounds. Built in
1899, the white house is
well maintained and
furnished. Special
celebrations during the
year.

Haas-Lilienthal House

2007 Franklin Street,
San Francisco,
(415) 441-3004
Built in 1886, the gray
house is a classic
storybook Victorian. The
fully furnished house was
lived in until 1972 when it
was donated to the
Foundation for San
Francisco's Architectural
Heritage.

Octagon House

2645 Gough Street,
San Francisco,
(415) 441-7512
Gray with white trim and
quoining, the house was
built in 1861, and is now a
Colonial museum set in a
quiet garden. Acquired in
1952 as their headquarters
by the California Colonial
Dames of America.

Whittier Mansion

2090 Jackson Street,
San Francisco,
(415) 567-1848
The 30-room
Richardsonian-Roman-
esque 1896 mansion was
fitted at the turn of the
century with gas-electric
fixtures and an Otis
elevator. Home of the
California Historical
Society.

Designer Ron Mann's *Shadow* vases are available in three sizes and finishes ranging from verdigris to sandcast bronze. Each has its own special character. Available from the Ron Mann Designs studio, 497 Carolina Street, (415) 864-4911 (Through a designer or architect).

DESIGN AND STYLE STORES

These stores are our top choices for an only-in-San Francisco treat. Superbly displayed merchandise, out-of-the-way locations, and unique points of view are here in spades, thanks to a savvy collection of local entrepreneurs. Brilliant, single-minded, visionary, hard-working, and idiosyncratic, these store owners make their businesses special and inspiring. Many of the stores sell handcrafts of Northern California you won't find elsewhere.

Accession

388 Hayes Street,
San Francisco,
(415) 861-3191
Handcrafted and antique
accessories. Antique
textiles and masks.

Aerial

The Cannery,
2801 Leavenworth Street,
San Francisco,
(415) 474-1566
The out-there owners sell
only what they love—an
ever-changing collection of
architectural prints, art
books, accessories, well-
designed sporting equip-
ment, and fun stuff. Water
bar. Store designed by
architect Richard Altuna.

Agraria

1156 Taylor Street,
San Francisco,
(415) 771-5922
Maurice Gibson and
Stanford Stevenson make
the most elegant potpourri
and soaps. A very chic
(and wonderfully
fragrant) store. Catalogue.

San Francisco designer David Best's sidetable of colorful laminate on wood from Limn, 457 Pacific Street, (415) 397-7474.

Pine table with tapered legs (48" by 24") crafted by Tony Cowan. Custom order this and other designs from The Cottage Table Company, 550 18th Street, (415) 957-1760.

Arch
407 Jackson Street,
San Francisco,
(415) 433-2724
Architect Susan Colliver's colorful, graphic store sells supplies for designers, architects, and artists. Fun place.

Bell'Occhio
8 Brady Street,
San Francisco,
(415) 864-4048
Claudia Schwartz and Toby Hanson hand-paint and sell ribbons, charming tableware, antiques, and wonderfully idiosyncratic treasures.

Bloomers
2975 Washington Street,
San Francisco,
(415) 563-3266
In an expansive new shop, bustling Bloomers sells glorious flowers, vases, ribbons, and baskets.

Virginia Breier
3091 Sacramento Street,
San Francisco,
(415) 929-7173
Also at Ghirardelli Square, 900 North Point Street, San Francisco, (415) 474-5036. A fine gallery for viewing contemporary and traditional American crafts, including furniture and tableware.

Builders Booksource
1817 4th Street,
Berkeley,
(415) 845-6874
With an accent on the practical, this well-stocked store includes books on interior design, gardens, architecture, and materials. Catalogue.

The Cottage Table Company
550 18th Street,
San Francisco,
(415) 957-1760
Craftsman Tony Cowan custom makes fine classic hardwood tables to order. A rare find. Shipping available. Catalogue.

Cottonwood
3461 Sacramento Street,
San Francisco,
(415) 346-6020
Well-edited Southwest style. Accent on beautiful craftsmanship.

Susan Cummins Gallery
32 Miller Avenue,
Mill Valley,
(415) 383-1512
Fine ceramics, crafts, and paintings.

Dandelion
2877 California Street,
San Francisco,
(415) 563-3100
Ostensibly a gift emporium, this superbly stocked store sells books, tableware, accessories, beautiful things.

Decorum
1632 Market Street,
San Francisco,
(415) 864-DECO
Impeccably restored authentic art deco and Moderne in an expansive store opposite the Zuni Cafe.

Fillamento
2185 Fillmore Street,
San Francisco,
(415) 931-2224
A neighborhood favorite. Style-concious furniture, tableware, rugs, and gifts.

Black leather "Oxford" club chair designed by Michael Vanderbyl for Bernhardt has small cast aluminum feet. Available through Risa Ogroskin Associates, 149 9th Street, San Francisco, 94103, (415) 552-0655.

Fioridella
1920 Polk Street,
San Francisco,
(415) 775-4065
Jean Thompson and Barbara Belloli sell the most beautiful flowers in a glorious store full of fragrant blossoms and new ideas.

Flush
245 11th Street,
San Francisco,
(415) 252-0245
Brand new. Interior designer Chuck Winslow and Rosemary Klebahn created a rich world of beautiful objects. Linens, furniture, antiques, Venetian glass.

Garden or indoor bench designed by San Francisco artist Buddy Rhodes in hand-packed pigmented concrete with a ground and sealed surface. This and other exclusive designs available through Buddy Rhodes studio, (415) 332-7310.

The Gardener
1836 4th Street,
Berkeley,
(415) 548-4545
Alta Tingle's superbly styled, sunny store mixes gardening supplies, stone-topped tables, books, tableware, rustic furniture and beautifully crafted accessories. Well worth the trip.

Gump's
250 Post Street,
San Francisco,
(415) 982-1616
A treasure chest of fine Orient-inspired lamps, timeless furniture, elegant tableware, and more; since 1861.

Japonesque
Crocker Galleria
(third level),
50 Post Street,
San Francisco,
(415) 398-8577
Also **Gallery Japonesque,**
824 Montgomery Street,
San Francisco,
(415) 391-8860
Koichi Hara celebrates the Japanese love of harmony, simplicity, refined beauty, and humble materials— and the spirit of his design gallery is entirely contemporary.

Kris Kelly
One Union Square,
San Francisco,
(415) 986-8822
Fine embellished linens.

Sue Fisher King
3067 Sacramento Street,
San Francisco,
(415) 922-7276
Sue King's linens and tableware are the finest and prettiest. A must-stop for accessories and gifts.

Limn Company
457 Pacific Street,
San Francisco,
(415) 397-7474
Contemporary furniture and lighting by over 300 manufacturers. Philippe Starck to le Corbusier and back.

Macys
Stockton and O'Farrell Streets,
San Francisco
(415) 397-3333
John Dickinson showed his first furniture collections (some pieces are now in the collection of the San Francisco Museum of Modern Art) for the 1978 opening of the Macys Interior Design Department. Today, this is one of the few downtown stores to offer a wide range of furnishings and accessories, along with consultation and design services.

Naomi's Antiques To Go
1207 Sutter Street,
San Francisco,
(415) 775-1207
Art pottery to the rafters! Bauer and Fiesta, of course, plus great finds.

Postmark
333 Bryant Street,
San Francisco,
(415) 243-9780
Lee Gamble and Michael Say buy the best Italian furniture and lighting, plus Atelier International lighting and furniture collections.

White linen-covered Doralice chairs by Flexform at Postmark, 333 Bryant Street, (415) 243-9780.

Digit I painted steel and glass table by San Francisco designer/craftsman Peter Gutkin. Also available in wood and laminate and custom finishes. Available to order from Peter Gutkin Design, 170 Capp Street, (415) 861-8848.

Santa Fe
3571 Sacramento Street, San Francisco, (415) 346-0180
Southwestern style for Californians. Fine Navaho rugs, Navaho silver, ranch furniture, photography.

Smith & Hawken
25 Corte Madera, Mill Valley, (415) 383-2000
The place for garden furniture, plants, garden tools, vases, seeds, and terra cotta pots. Fine catalogue.

Tail of the Yak
2632 Ashby Avenue, Berkeley, (415) 841-9891
Partners Alice Hoffman Erb and Lauren Adams Allard have created an entrancing store that is always a treat. Decorative accessories, Mexican furniture, fabrics, and antique jewelry. Colorful, and full of ideas.

20th Century
1612 Market Street, San Francisco, (415) 626-0524
Modernist furniture by American designers from 1925 through the fifties.

Vanderbilt & Co
1429 Main Street, St. Helena, (707) 963-1010
This is where San Franciscans with houses in the Napa Valley shop for accessories for the bedroom, kitchen, and tabletop. Damask and Jacquard table linens.

Vignette
3625 Sacramento Street, San Francisco, (415) 567-0174
In a new store designed by architect Steve MacCracken, pretty accessories, contemporary furniture, linens.

La Ville Du Soleil
444 Post Street, San Francisco, (415) 398-8646
Opera lover Lillian Williams also loves France. Everything for the Francophile, including tableware, furniture, and linens.

Williams-Sonoma
150 Post Street, San Francisco, (415) 362-6904
Flagship for the Williams-Sonoma cookware empire. Also a fine collection of delicacies. Catalogue.

William Stout Architectural Books
804 Montgomery, San Francisco, (415) 391-6757
Architect Bill Stout's store specializes in obscure twentieth-century publications, along with new and out-of-print books. Catalogue.

Zia
6026 College Avenue, Oakland, (415) 652-4647
Artist Colin Smith's wonderful store looks to the Southwest and sells an artful and colorful collection of hands-on furnishings and accessories. Navaho textiles.

A SELECTION OF ANTIQUE STORES

W. Graham Arader III
560 Sutter Street, San Francisco, (415) 788-5115
Californiana, maps, the American West engravings, lithographs, oils.

Bauer Antiques
1878 Union Street, San Francisco, (415) 921-7656
French and Continental furniture, eighteenth and nineteenth centuries.

Challis House
463 Jackson Street, San Francisco, (415) 397-6999
Fine furniture and works of art.

San Francisco's antique dealers travel the world to bring back treasures for their stores. This Swedish neo-classic tall-case clock, *right,* from Therien & Co., Inc., 411 Vermont Street, (415) 956-8850.

The refurbished Monadnock Building, 685 Market Street, offers many pleasures to the visitor. There are the John Berggruen and Modernism galleries, along with virtuoso painting in the lobby and courtyard by San Francisco's Evans & Brown. The ten-story courtyard was painted in *trompe l'oeil* architecture in the style of Italian Renaissance revival with a dash of Beaux Arts. Photograph by Peter Christiansen.
Painting by Charles Brown and Mark Evans, Evans & Brown Studio, 1451 Stevenson Street, (415) 255-2735.

Evelyne Conquaret Antiques
Showplace Square West,
550 15th Street,
San Francisco,
(415) 552-6100
Eighteenth- and nineteenth-century French antiques.

Dillingham and Company
470 Jackson Street,
San Francisco,
(415) 989-8777
English antique furniture and accessories.

Robert Domergue & Company
560 Jackson Street,
San Francisco,
(415) 781-4034
Seventeenth- and eighteenth-century French furniture.

John Doughty Antiques
619 Sansome Street,
San Francisco,
(415) 398-6849
Seventeenth-, eighteenth-, and early nineteenth-century English and French furniture and accessories.

Drum & Company
415 Jackson Street,
San Francisco,
(415) 788-5118
Eighteenth-century English, Continental furniture.

Louis D. Fenton Antiques
432 Jackson Street,
San Francisco,
(415) 398-3046
Fine selection of antiques.

Charles William Gaylord Antiques
2151 Powell Street,
San Francisco,
(415) 392-6085
Fine French antiques, superb mantels.

Foster Gwin Inc.
425 Jackson Street,
San Francisco,
(415) 397-4986
Period English, Oriental, and Continental furniture.

Ed Hardy
750 Post Street,
San Francisco,
(415) 771-6644
Continental and Oriental antiques.

Hawley Bragg
3364 Sacramento Street,
San Francisco,
(415) 563-8122
Antiques, interior design.

Robert Hering
3307 Sacramento Street,
San Francisco,
(415) 563-4144
English and Continental antiques, interior design.

Kuromatsu
722 Bay Street,
San Francisco,
(415) 474-4027
Japanese *mingei, tansu, ikebana* baskets.

Lyons Ltd, Antique Prints
2700 Hyde Street,
San Francisco,
(415) 441-2202
Original period graphics from 1490 to 1900.

Norman Shepherd
458 Jackson Street,
San Francisco,
(415) 362-4145
Seventeenth-, eighteenth-, and nineteenth-century English, Continental furniture.

Shibata Art Studio
3028 Fillmore Street,
San Francisco,
(415) 567-1530
A treasure house of Oriental antiques. Wonderful ambiance.

Glen W. Smith Galleries
2021 Fillmore Street,
San Francisco,
(415) 931-3081
Eclectic, international antiques.

Therien & Co. Inc.
411 Vermont Street,
San Francisco,
(415) 956-8850
Seventeenth- and eighteenth-century English, North European, and Continental furniture.

Walker McIntyre Antiques
3615 Sacramento Street,
San Francisco,
(415) 563-8024
English, Continental, and American antiques.

WALKING TOURS:

Architectural Tours
Foundation for San Francisco's Architectural Heritage, 2007 Franklin Street (Haas-Lilienthal House), offers a variety of walks and tours year-round. Telephone (415) 441-3000 for information.

Art Deco Tours
The Art Deco Society of California conducts walking tours of the Marina, plus a shopping tour of the City's art deco shops. Telephone (415) 552-DECO for information.

Chinatown Tours
Docent-guided heritage and architecture walks through San Francisco's Chinatown. Daily tours from the Chinese Cultural Center, 750 Kearny Street. Telephone (415) 986-1822 for reservations.

City Guides
Free one-hour walks of historic Market Street, the old Gold Rush City, City Hall, and the Civic Center. Telephone (415) 558-3981 for information.

Ciao lacquered table, *above,* designed by Gary Hutton available from the Trimarco Showroom, Showplace Square West, 550 15th Street, (415) 552-7270 (To the trade).

FURNITURE SHOWROOMS:

Design Center
The handsome brick buildings in the area of the City around 15th Street at Kansas Street house more than 300 to-the-trade-only furniture, fabric, antique, and accessories showrooms. At the Galleria Design Center, the Showplace Design Center, Showplace Square West, 200 Kansas—and in Jackson Square—the wares of all the prestigious manufacturers are presented. Access may be arranged through an interior designer, architect, or contractor.

San Francisco designer Orlando Diaz-Azcuy's *Athenee* chair for HBF. Inspired by seventeenth-century furniture, its curvy lines suggest grace and refinement. Available through Offices Unlimited, 444 Spear Street, (415) 543-4440 (To the trade).

INDEX